Confessions of
A Dad

My Kids Don't Understand The Value of Money

AZHAR LAHER

Published by
First edition.
Website Designer: Sean Mitchell
Cover Designer: Kevin Monk
Cover art: Kevin Monk
ISBN-13: 9781512028386
ISBN-10: 151202838X

DEDICATION

This book is dedicated to my brilliant, thoughtful and beautiful wife. She never complains or interferes, asks nothing, and dedicates her life to support others. She also writes my dedications.

To my children, who will inherit this world and make it a much better place.

To my mother – you are the strongest woman I know

To my father – you taught me the value of knowledge

As Rascal Flatts sang:

"My Wish"

My wish for you is that this life becomes all that you want it to.

Your dreams stay big; your worries stay small.

You never need to carry more than you can hold.

And while you're out there gettin' where you're gettin' to,

I hope you know somebody loves you.

And wants the same things, too.

Yeah, this is my wish.

I hope you never look back and you never forget.

All the ones who love you and the place you left

I hope you always forgive and you never regret.

And you help somebody every chance you get.

Oh, you find God's grace, in every mistake,

And always give more than you take.

But more than anything, yeah, more than anything

My wish, for you, is that this life becomes all that you want it to,

—Steele, Robson, 2006

ACKNOWLEDGMENTS

This book has taken me several years to write, in part because of how much the world of personal finance has changed within such a short time. While writing, I had so many conversations with so many people that it is difficult to know where to begin giving thanks, but the obvious place to start is with my two children, Nazeefah and Nabeel, who provided the inspiration for what you are about to read. My wife Fatima is my life and my inspiration. Thank you, Fatima, for your words of wisdom, encouragement, and gentle criticism.

Dr. Mariam Vania-Bulbulia, an amazing and inspirational soul, thank you for providing insights and writing the foreword.

Courtney Carroll has generously given his time over the years for significant discussions about the direction this manuscript should take. Members of the Thornhill Wealth Forum, (www.thornhillwealthforum. com) have inspired me with their stories of success and failure since 2007.

Matt Scherb has taught me so much about integrity and treating people the way I want to be treated. Gordon So, thank you for infusing your entrepreneurial spirit into every conversation.

Ashraf Zaghloul, you have inspired my thinking and allowed me to dig deep into my understanding of the "big picture."

Best-selling author Rachel Oliver helped me with her candor, her honesty, and her deep desire to make this book a success.

And while they may never know it, Matt Galloway, Sook-Yin Lee, Stuart Maclean, Rex Murphy and the staff at CBC Radio have deeply enriched my "offline" thinking time during long hours spent driving.

Cindy Prescher: as an editor, your vision introduced me to new viewpoints and sharpened my thinking. It has been an immense pleasure to work with you.

Sean Mitchell: your creative spark with the website development and trailer video has opened the book to a wider audience. It has been an honor working with you.

David: Thank goodness for your editing skills and eye for detail.

I especially want to thank those close to me who patiently endured my fascination with personal finance and living a contented life—my dear parents, siblings, cousins and friends.

And one final note, just for Nazeefah and Nabeel: I wrote this book so that you two could grow up with more "common cents" than I did!

Azhar Laher
Thornhill, Ontario
May 2015

TABLE OF CONTENTS

FOREWORD

Making the decision to have a child—it's momentous. It
is to decide forever to have your heart go walking around
outside your body.

— Elizabeth Stone

The goal of this book has nothing to do with accumulating wealth, but everything to do with helping my children, and yours, to understand money and to develop healthy habits about money. I love my kids too much to let them develop bad money habits that could haunt them throughout their lives. Warren Buffett said, "Chains of habit are too light to be felt until they're too heavy to be broken." I sincerely want my kids to recognize good habits while they are still young, before their patterns become chains that bind them.

Although parents protect their kids from all sorts of destructive behavior while they are still living at home, some parents neglect to teach their children how to manage money or how to develop healthy financial habits. Without even realizing, parents may neglect to teach their children the very skills necessary to avert personal and financial ruin.

Personal finance and basic money management is generally not emphasized in school, so the responsibility for teaching this touchy topic falls squarely upon the shoulders of parents.

There are several reasons why parents may not follow through on this responsibility. Some parents may feel their children will figure out "money stuff" on their own, as they live their lives. While this may be partially true, there is no reason to let your kids drown for lack of understanding when you have within you the ability to help prevent it. If handed a car and a car key, most teenagers could eventually figure out how to drive, but no sane parent would let their child risk injury and death learning how to drive by trial and error.

Kids who don't receive basic guidance about financial matters have the potential of suffering some hefty bumps and bruises in life. We parents must remember that the responsibility for educating our kids about personal finance is always with us—even after our kids finish school and transition into their early young adult years.

Most parents live in a constant state of overload. Many parents are struggling to meet work, financial, social, and family obligations that require them to have the energy of the Energizer Bunny. It is easier for parents to throw their hands up in the air and say, "I don't have time! Let the school do it – that's what we pay teachers for."

Well, guess what? The teachers are saying, "It's not our responsibility. We are overworked and underpaid. Let the parents teach their own children about money." Folks, it doesn't take a rocket scientist to see that when the pass-the-buck attitude prevails, it is our children who stand to lose the most.

And let's be honest: parents can be lousy teachers. Maybe it's because their own parents were lousy teachers. No matter the reason, the cycle will continue until someone breaks it. That someone should be *you*! The first step you can take is to stop and take a good look at what you have (or have not) taught your children about money. When my wife and I decided that we needed to change the way our kids managed money, we realized that we were doing the opposite of what we should have been doing. Instead of teaching our children sound financial habits, we had helped them develop bad ones. Here are some of the ways that we had unwittingly fostered such negative patterns.

We gave them everything they wanted in life.

Most parents who were not indulged in their own childhood want their children to have the Best of everything. We told ourselves that they were still young and should simply enjoy life. Who cares if it meant spoiling them a little bit along the way – they would have the rest of their lives to master money.

We fostered an entitlement mentality.

By purposely not teaching our kids that they should expect to work hard to get what they want, we inadvertently trained them to believe that whatever they wanted should naturally be given to them. After talking with other parents, I realized that this is a common problem for parents who give freely to their children. This type of dynamic leads children to develop an expectation that they will always be given what they want!

We ignored the importance of budgeting.

The word "budget" was never part of our dinner table vocabulary. It is quite possible, in fact, that my own children have never spoken the word! Were it not for the fact that they are intelligent kids, I might wonder if they know the word exists! This is also a common problem for people who aren't forced to live on a budget.

We gave the impression that saving is only for retirement.

Our overindulging gave our kids the impression that it was OK to spend whatever money they were given without saving any of it: we had showed them that money was, and always would be, plentiful. Kids need to know that saving part of their money is a good way to obtain the big things that they want in life. It brings them a sense of satisfaction to know they worked, saved, sacrificed, and got something for themselves. When our kids were young, we robbed them of all that by not teaching them how to save.

Fortunately, it's not too late! There's still time to teach our children about money. We can show them healthy spending and saving habits, a work ethic, and how to invest their money. I imagine there are many other parents out there who still have the time to help their kids understand money and set them on a healthy path. In addition to serving as a guide for my own kids, this book is also intended for all the other parents and children who know that it is best to develop good, lifelong habits when you are young. So, let us get started!

Dr. Mariam Vania-Bulbulia, Child and adolescent psychiatrist, Toronto.

INTRODUCTION

The beginning is the most important part of the work.

— PLATO

One lesson that we neglected to teach our children is the concept of financial freedom.

To be fair, my wife and I had spent countless hours reminding our children about the value of a good education. We focused tremendous efforts on instilling good morals and values, and we spoke often about the importance of having strong, healthy relationships with family, friends, and neighbors. We talked about respect, humility, and community service. All of these were consistent topics for sit-down conversations in our household.

But what we missed was sitting down and formally teaching our kids about the importance of good financial habits and the true value of financial freedom. We assumed that our son and daughter would learn these skills via osmosis — you know, the way they usually learn about sex through their friends and older cousins. Well, as it turns out, sex may be an interesting topic that friends and cousins discuss, but money? Not so much. It's rarely even a topic of discussion among their generation, except for complaining that they deserve more.

It is our responsibility to teach our children about managing their money, saving, and investing for the future. We cannot depend on anyone else to do it. The schools don't do a good job of raising a child's financial IQ. While many kids learn about the birds and the bees through casual conversation around the dinner table, peers, books, and television, how many of them learn about managing their money though TV? Not many.

The comments our kids make explain to us why they don't easily learn about money in the same way they learn about other things. Some of the things they say are:

- ❖ "This money stuff is boring."
- ❖ "I know my parents will take care of anything that has to do with money."
- ❖ "I don't earn money, so I don't really need to know all of that stuff."
- ❖ "I'll learn about money when I'm older. I have too many other things I want to do now while I'm young."

(Does it ever occur to our children that if they learn about money now, it could actually give them more freedom to do what they want to do later?) To me, this is like saying, "I want to eat absurd amounts of cake and ice cream every day, and I'll worry about cutting back after I'm so overweight that I can't easily exercise!"

We have tried to give our kids practical advice such as:

- ❖ "Be careful where you spend your hard-earned money."

"Spend your money on practical, useful things and meaningful experiences, not on designer fads that have no value and quickly fade away like yesterday's garbage."

I wonder if they ever stop to consider the absurdity of trying to keep up with a fashion industry that releases a different fashion line every few months. Don't they ever get sick of chasing after the newest fashion statement, only to have to repeat the process the next month? This father is scratching his head over that one!

That old cliché of parents not wanting to deprive their children of anything because they were deprived while growing up certainly resonates in my family. Though we sometimes even realize we could be doing our kids a disservice, the guilt of saying "no" can sometimes be simply too much to bear. Of course we want to indulge our children and make their dreams come true. And let's be honest – it makes Mommy and Daddy look great, too! Who doesn't want that?

As children become teenagers, the problem only deepens. We want to remain on their minds during their busy lives, even if the thought occurs mainly because we just spent a fortune for them at the mall. We want to be their "hero" presenting them with the perfect gift that helps them be more trendy and popular at school.

Admittedly, we also worried what our friends and family might say if our kids didn't keep up with the trends. It's true: we caved to peer pressure, the very thing we tell our children to resist doing. "Stay true to your standards," we remind them in moments of wanting to fit in with the crowd, "it's OK to be different."

But when it comes to finances, kids catch on very quickly that their parents want to look like they have it all. Teenagers aren't the only ones who want to fit in, after all: Mommy and Daddy want to keep up with the Joneses, too.

It's not that I want my children to become financial experts. Their lives can be rich and rewarding without them becoming personal finance gurus. But money is a tool that must be used wisely and skillfully, and I want to teach my kids how to use it. In order to live the financially secure lives that I want for them, they must have a basic understanding of money. It's simply unavoidable.

The purpose of this book is twofold. First, it is an attempt to help equip parents with the skills and knowledge necessary to educate their children (and themselves). For parents who simply do not know what to say to their kids about money, this book will serve as a guide.

The book also includes personal letters that I have written to my children, Nazeefah and Nabeel. These notes contain heartfelt instructions about the concepts that I hope they can learn, and then apply, within their own lives. My hope is that these letters will resonate with parents and help kids realize that they are not alone when it comes to the difficulty of understanding money.

I recognize that families have limited amounts time in today's busy world. And this is something I kept in mind at the very heart of this book's design. As you will see, I have intentionally divided the chapters into short segments for those who read on the go – which seems to be just about everyone these days. It's my hope that the brevity will also appeal to preteens and teens, who always seem to have something better to do than listen while Mom and Dad talk about Important Things.

I truly believe that once our children have learned the core concepts of personal finance, they will have the tools they need to be financially free.

This is my driving inspiration in writing this book.

PART ONE: THE IMPORTANT STUFF IN YOUR LIFE

We rush through our days with so much to do, so much
we should be doing, so much we're missing out on … but
how often do we stop to appreciate the place where we
are right now?

— LEO BABAUTA

1

PARENTS, GET REAL!

Do not educate your child to be rich. Educate him to be
happy, so that when he grows up he will know the value
of things, not the price.

— UNKNOWN

Like anything else in life, we are able to accomplish good things when we
choose to be honest with ourselves and get down to the real work of getting things done. Here are some honest thoughts and ideas about getting
real with your kids about money. The concepts are general, but you can
adapt them to fit your family's situation and specific needs.

Teach what you know to be right, not necessarily what your parents taught you.

Before you embark on the journey to teach your children about finances,
make sure to clarify your own financial understanding. Educate yourself –
after all, how can you teach that which you don't know? Even worse, how
can you be a good example if you don't practice what you preach? Kids
quickly pick up on inconsistencies between what their parents say and

what they do. While our own parents may have gotten by with ordering us to "do as I say, not as I do," today's generation of children is far too critical to accept this line of reasoning – not that this is a bad thing, of course.

With this in mind, **Part 4** of the book outlines resources to help you jump-start your own education.

Live what you teach.

Exemplify the financial principles you want to instill within your children. When children see what you *do*, versus what you *say*, they have "Aha!" moments that will stay with them for a lifetime. Find opportunities to demonstrate financial lessons in everyday life.

Understand that you are not doing your children any favors by neglecting to teach them financial responsibility.

Have you ever heard an adult say, "I wish my parents had *NOT* taught me about finances?" Of course you haven't. Those who are fortunate enough to have had parents who taught them about money tend to be grateful for the advantages it has given them. Many people who are financially successful attribute their success to the lessons about money they learned from parents and other role models.

Don't be afraid to say no.

No matter what your relationship is with your children, it can be scary to say no to them! Saying no to a child makes a parent's heart hurt, especially when big, beautiful eyes and abundant tears are involved. Parents may experience a twinge of pain when saying no leads their children to tears. Even worse, words of rejection from children can bring the strongest parent to their knees in an instant. Oh, the sting of a child's voice shouting, "I don't like you anymore!" But this is when it's most important to remember that a simple, resolute no could be the best learning experience your child ever has.

Let kids be involved in household finances.

Understanding how household expenses work helps kids appreciate the reality that money is earned through hard work, and then must first be allotted for our needs. It's important to show them that things like toys and other luxuries cost money, which must be earned. Understanding this will help engage your children in financial responsibility and, learning to not be wasteful.

Create age-appropriate, real-life scenarios that involve your children.

Kids can sometimes be oblivious to how much food, utilities, household items, and personal hygiene items cost. Get them involved in thinking about finances in fun ways: for instance, have them plan a meal to cook, beginning with making the grocery list, and shopping for the ingredients with you. Have them keep track of the price of each item so that they can learn how much it costs to prepare the meal. You can also show your kids the utility bills and ask them to write out the checks for those bills for a month. Exercises like this may help them to develop an appreciation for the financial resources needed to have running water, electricity, heating, and cooling.

Let kids learn from their mistakes.

Nothing can be harder for a parent than watching their children struggle or fail at something. Every fiber of our being roots for our kids to succeed! Indeed, it goes against our very nature to allow them to make mistakes. But sometimes, making their own mistakes is the best way to learn lasting, lifelong lessons.

If you give your child an allowance and they spend it all immediately, they should suffer the consequences when they realize they want to spend money on something else instead. If you give in when they beg for more money, you instead risk showing your child that there are no consequences for spending money thoughtlessly. It is a true disservice to children when they learn this bad habit from enabling parents and carry it into their adult lives.

It's likely that some of the best lessons you learned growing up were when your parents allowed you to make mistakes that had a significant impact on your thinking. Don't deny your children these lessons. They may be painful, but they are invaluable!

Do not ignore sound financial principles because of your own childhood.

As adults, we have to accept the fact that our childhoods were what they were and our children must live their own lives. Even if we lacked the essentials in life as children, we must remember not to overcompensate with our own children. On the other hand, if we had wealthy, overindulgent parents and we developed a distaste for material possessions, we do not help our children by telling them that money is evil and that they must sacrifice all material possessions in order to be good people. When it comes to teaching our kids about money, we must leave our childhood triumphs and wounds behind. We must teach our children financial balance and freedom based on sound principles, not emotions.

Don't foster an entitlement mentality.

We hear the word "entitlement" often these days. Many people have forgotten the value of working hard for what they get. Other, more malignant individuals may even take advantage of others' generosity rather than put in any honest work themselves. More than ever before, even the wealthiest of parents should teach their children to earn their keep and become independent through hard work.

Once the seed of entitlement is planted in children, earning money to buy what they want can seem like an irrelevant chore to them. They may ask you, "but why do I have to work to buy what I want when you can just give it to me?" And let's be honest – if children have been taught to feel entitled all their lives, this kind of question shouldn't be surprising.

Once entitled children grow up and enter the corporate world, they may be in for a shock when the world refuses to give them anything for free. It is the responsibility of parents to prepare their children for the real world.

Show your children that budgeting is important, no matter the family's financial status.

It may be difficult for children to understand why a budget is important when there seems to be an endless supply of money at home. Budgeting might seem like something only poor people do – or worse, children may not even know what budgeting is at all. The responsibility of teaching that money is never limitless rests squarely on the shoulders of parents.

It's a natural tendency for kids to feel like the universe revolves around them. In some extremes, it might even seem like Mom and Dad's money exists for the purpose of pleasing them. Parents must continually remind their children that this is not the case, and that it is important to share with those who are less fortunate.

It's important for children to learn the difference between living frugally and being cheap. Parents need to help kids understand that there is nothing wrong or shameful about living frugally, even when a family's wealth does not necessitate doing so.

Teach that saving is fundamental.

Don't assume that your kids will naturally be savers or have an inherent understanding of why saving is important. Kids sometimes have a difficult time relating to the future. They are more inclined to live in the here and now than their parents and elders. Take the time to show them. Encourage your children to set aside a portion of any money they receive. They may not like having rules about money now, but as they grow older they will appreciate that you helped them begin saving early.

Remember – it's much easier to learn good habits from the start than to break bad ones! If they begin the process of saving in childhood, it will be natural for them to continue this habit into adulthood.

Teach modesty about wealth and possessions.

In a society where wealth is seen as a testament of success, it can be tempting to use money and possessions to create an image for oneself. This is true for both parents and children. Everyone, after all, can be vulnerable to peer pressure. As a parent, you must instill a sense of self-worth in your children that extends far beyond the trappings of wealth. Show them how to find their self-worth from within. We want our children to live healthy, happy, authentic lives. If their lives are built upon impressing others, this will not happen. Kids should learn this lesson early.

Teach about finances organically.

Along with some structured teaching, be sure to leave room for impromptu, "teachable moments" about finance whenever the opportunity arises – these often occur at the most unexpected times.

Use real-life examples, like stories from the media, anecdotes from people your children can relate to, interesting quotes, and so forth. Unless you want your kids to hide whenever they see you coming, don't bombard them with a new lesson every time you talk to them! Find ways to teach them life lessons without making them feel that they are in school.

Let your children know your motivations for teaching them about finances.

The bottom line is that you are teaching your children about money because of your love and concern for their future. They should know that your desire is for them to live a successful, happy life. If they don't understand this, they may resent your teaching, or even rebel against it.

Contrary to what you may tell your kids, parents are human and make mistakes! That means that sometimes our motives are a bit off. Perhaps you are known for your financial intelligence, and you boast about your kid's financial savvy. Even though you should not ignore teaching your children humility about wealth, they may sense that your financial talks are motivated by your desire to turn them into a financial whiz kid. But that can be a good thing.

Final Thoughts

Parents:

Take the opportunity to teach your children about money, both formally and throughout your daily routines. If it seems as though your kids are disinterested, keep teaching! They absorb more than you know. The payoff may not come immediately, but it will happen. Think of it like all of those expensive trips to the orthodontist—for several years, all you see are wires on the teeth and huge bills, but the day will come when all you'll notice is a beautiful smile!

—AL

2

KIDS, GET REAL

Learn from the mistakes of others. You can never live
long enough to make them all yourself.

— GROUCHO MARX

Kids of all ages, your moms and dads have been given the great responsibility to help teach you the skills for living the best life possible. More than anything, your parents want you to be happy and healthy. It thrills them to see you engaged in productive activities that will help you become well-adjusted adults. That's just the nature of being a parent!

Your parents know that if you learn certain things, you are likely to make good decisions that will enrich your life. That's why they want to teach you about money and financial freedom. I know, it probably isn't your favorite subject, but the time will come when you are glad they showed you these things.

Read the thoughts that follow and think about them. If you can learn to see your family's finances in the same light as they do, you can enjoy learning about it together. Your parents can teach you all kinds of things about money.

Below is just a short list of the many things they can teach you.

Money doesn't grow on trees.

In most cases, your parents have had to do something to get the money they have. They have worked, planned, saved, invested wisely, and followed sound financial principles. But no matter how they got their money, one thing is certain—it didn't magically appear for them. Your mom and dad don't have a limitless amount of money, either.

Your parents have wisely managed their money in order to maintain their financial status. They could have spent it on fancy restaurants and vacations without a second thought, but they didn't, and here's why: they had the future of their family in mind. Understand this as they teach you to do the same.

Money might not be as "boring" as you think.

When you're young, you may crave constant excitement. Learning about finances might seem boring! Fair enough. But finances don't have to fall into the "ignore" category either. There's probably lots of ways money could be interesting to you. Maybe you just haven't thought about it yet. But your parents have – and they want to share them with you.

Like it or not, money is an important part of life, and you need to understand it well beyond the contents of your wallet. You're smart in other areas of your life. Being smart about money can work out well for you!

The more you know about money, the more you can use it to your benefit. What's boring about that? If you really want to become an independent grownup, you'll need to know enough about money to manage yours by yourself. If you can't, your independence from Mom and Dad could be short lived – you could even find yourself having to move back home. Now, *that* could be boring!

Don't let yourself feel entitled.

The definition of entitlement is assuming the right to receive certain guaranteed benefits without earning them first. If you start to believe that you are guaranteed certain monetary benefits just because you exist, or just because your parents have the money, you will miss out on some of life's most rewarding experiences. You'll miss learning to live a life of gratitude, learning to earn what you have, and learning to appreciate how hard your parents have worked to provide you with material possessions.

Keep in mind that your parents owe you nothing, but strive to give you everything that you need (and much of what you want, too). Your parents give you things because they want to bless you. Rather than feel entitled to what you are given, remember to be grateful for it.

Develop healthy attitudes and money habits while you are still young.

Money isn't an old-person topic; it is an every-person topic. Those who have wealth and financial freedom later on in life are those who developed healthy money habits when they were kids. Learn how to save, invest, and manage your money so that it serves you and others.

Don't use money to manipulate, impress, or establish your identity.

I devote a greater proportion of this book to the false identity that money can provide because it is an important topic. But always try to keep money in its proper perspective and use it for good. Remember, money only has the power that you give it. You can give it the power to accomplish positive or negative things. Your life can become warped and out of balance if you give money too much power or use in the wrong ways. Think of the powers that superheroes have. With all that power, they can choose to either do wonderful things, or great harm. Determine in your heart that you will use money for good, and carry it out in your actions.

Remember — money isn't your identity. What you have does NOT make you who you are. Money is just something in your possession, nothing more. Having a castle doesn't make the owner a king or queen. And having an expensive sports car does not make you more attractive to the opposite sex (or it shouldn't at least). It just makes you the same person that you are already — except with a sports car in the driveway.

Focus on becoming the person you really want to be and use your knowledge about money to help you reach the goals you want to reach. Think of it this way—if your identity is determined by how much money you have, what would happen if you woke up one morning and all of your money had vanished? Who would you be then?

Your parents' motivation is their love and concern for you.

Your parents don't have a secret agenda to turn you into some kind of financial tycoon. Believe me – parents don't want to have Donald Trump for a kid! Your parents want to help you achieve healthy, independent living and financial sustainability – that's it! There's no hidden motive. Your parents think about the future and know that the time will come when they will no longer walk on this earth with you. They know that if they succeed at teaching you the skills you need to be a successful, independent adult, you will be OK.

Parents want to know that they have taught you well and that you will live a good life when they are gone. Give them that reassurance by listening to what they have to say.

Final Thoughts

Dear Nazeefah and Nabeel,

The best time to learn about managing money is when you are young. Your mother and I have learned through trial and error and have made many mistakes along the way. Although it may not seem like it now, we have a lot to teach you – and the best time to start is now. Your mother and I are smarter than you think! We have experience on our side.

Your best interests are always at the forefront of my mind.
Dad

3

MONEY CAN'T BUY HAPPINESS

Try not to become a man of success, but rather try to
become a man of value.

— ALBERT EINSTEIN

Confession #1

As my kids saw it, joy and happiness came from having a few extra dollars and, not from enjoying positive experiences and meaningful relationships. It never occurred to them to find happiness in the simple things in life. Maybe it was too obvious, too easy to overlook. A rich life full of happiness has very little to do with money. You can be happy for a lifetime, with or without wealth.

Money can elicit all kinds of emotions, but it does not bring long-term happiness. Happiness, it turns out, simply can't be bought. And when people do try to buy happiness, the end result is often a vicious cycle of debt. Advertisers, with their clever use of emotionally appealing imagery, would have us believe that acquiring certain things is the clue to happiness. The truth is, falling into debt in pursuit of happiness simply makes things worse for an already-unhappy person, because the burdens we carry as we try to reduce our debt bring no enjoyment to our lives. Happiness cannot be bought. This can be a tough lesson for some people to learn.

The dictionary defines *money* as something that is accepted as a medium of exchange. In other words, money is something that you give in order to get something in return, such as products or services. The dictionary describes *happiness* as the state of feeling pleasure and contentment. The words money and happiness are not interchangeable. How can something like a medium of exchange buy the feeling of pleasure and contentment? The answer is simple – it can't. If you are not happy without money, you will not be happy with money.

The majority of people in the world are not wealthy. But it is ridiculous to think that all of these people are unhappy. Many of these people choose to be happy, and they find pleasure in things that have nothing to do with money. You can, too!

George Carlin once said, "Trying to be happy by accumulating possessions is like trying to satisfy hunger by taping sandwiches all over your body." External things cannot feed your soul any more than food on the outside of the body can feed the stomach. Too often, people waste their lives in foolish pursuit of money and possessions. Money can buy things that bring us temporary enjoyment, but once a desire is satisfied, another always arises.

Many people seek money, thinking that it will bring them happiness. They forget about money's ugly side: greed and unhealthy financial habits can lead to serious problems in one's life. People overspend on things they cannot afford. In the process, they often enter into debt and then live stressful lives of slaving away to pay off this debt. People like this have allowed their abuse of money to enslave them and rob them of their freedom.

Money can be used to feed addictions that people believe will make them happy. Addictions should be dealt with, not fed, because in the end, they enslave people just as money does. It shouldn't be hard to see the common thread between seeking happiness through money and the loss of freedom. Greed for "quick" money can lead to addictions like gambling.

Gambling is a rampant problem in modern society, often driving good people down a deceptive path that destroys their lives.

So, if money and all the things it buys cannot bring happiness, what does? Science tells us that people are happiest when they experience meaningful times and relationships. Having meaningful relationships with family and friends, being in robust mental and physical health, and feeling a strong purpose and passion in life are the true ingredients to happiness. These pleasures can be experienced whether or not a person has money.

Final Thoughts

Dear Nazeefah and Nabeel,

A wise man once said, "You don't have to be rich to find happiness." You may think that if you have money, happiness will automatically follow. But on the contrary, happiness is a choice — a choice that has nothing to do with how much money you posses. If happiness is linked to money, then it follows that all poor people are unhappy. However, many people who are not wealthy are nevertheless very happy. While on vacation in South Africa, I saw many people who could only afford to have one meal per day, but they were not unhappy. They smiled, laughed, and played soccer. They simply decided to be happy, and that is why they were happy.

Love,
Dad

4

MONEY AND RELATIONSHIPS

If you want to feel rich, just count the things you have
that money can't buy.

— EPICURUS

Confession #2

*My kids thought the essence of building and nurturing relationships was based on one's
financial status. They didn't realize how materialism influenced their relationships.*

Issues surrounding money seep into all parts of our lives, including
(or, perhaps I should say, especially) our relationships. Lack of communication about financial matters is one of the top ten reasons for divorce.
While money can be used to bless and help others, it can also be used to
manipulate and control. Conflicts over money and different opinions on
finance can ruin families and friendships.

Teens report that money definitely influences how they are treated at
school. Kids from poor families are often seen as lesser human beings
simply because of their financial status, because they don't wear high-end
clothing, and because they don't show off the latest technological devices.

How absurd is it to think that a poor person lacks the capacity to be a wonderful person and friend?

The right thing to do is to value people and healthy relationships above money and things. Doing so entails valuing people for who they are, not for what they have. Lasting relationships are built on mutual trust, respect, enjoyment of each other's company, and consideration for the other person's feelings. None of these foundations have anything to do with money. Forming a friendship based on money devalues the entire relationship.

Furthermore, choosing relationships based on money can cause people to live unauthentic lifestyles. This can entail living beyond one's means, while for others it can lead to trying to hide wealth. In either case, this obviously creates problems. It is best to be honest about your financial status, without being ashamed of it or flaunting it, and to live an authentic life regardless of your status. If others criticize you for hanging out with people outside your financial status, that is their problem, not yours. If you realize that a person is hanging out with you based on your financial status, have an honest talk with him or her and express your desire for an authentic relationship with a solid foundation, not one based on money.

There are times when we become friends with people in a different financial world than our own. You can ensure that the relationship between yourself and the other person proceeds as smoothly as possibly by keeping in mind a few rules of thumb.

- ❖ Be honest about your financial status and encourage the other person to do so as well.
- ❖ Plan money-neutral activities when possible. If you're the one with greater financial means, don't assume you should always pay for activities like eating out and so on; if you do, the other person may feel like he or she is accepting charity. Instead, plan low-cost activities, and occasionally treat your companion.
- ❖ If you are the person with less money, do not assume that the person with money will pay, shower you with gifts, and so forth just because he or she has more financial resources. That is not what the friendship is about.

❖ Never use your financial status to control or manipulate another person. Always treat the other person with the same level of respect and consideration with which you would treat him or her if you did not know that person's financial status.

Do not show off and brag about your possessions. Consider how it could make the other person feel. Besides, no one likes a braggart.

❖ When you give to the other person, give graciously, discreetly, and without ulterior motives.

Final Thoughts

Dear Nazeefah and Nabeel,

You are both amazing people and capable of building and maintaining deep, meaningful relationships no matter your financial status. Financial status should never determine relationships, how you treat other people, or how you allow them to treat you. You are worthy of relationships that are based on mutual respect and deep care. The characteristics and virtues that make someone a worthy friend have nothing to do with money. Choose your relationships carefully and do not let a person's finances influence your choices.

Sincerely,

Dad

5

LIVE WITH INTEGRITY AND VALUE YOUR CHARACTER

Spend your money on the things money can buy. Spend
your time on the things money can't buy.

—HARUKI MURAKAMI

Confession #3

*Growing up, my kids believed that you could only live a rich life if you had money. They
failed to realize that a life comprising good character and values is indeed a life richly
lived.*

Some things are far more valuable than money; your character and
integrity are two such examples. You can earn money, waste it, and earn
more yet again, but squander your character and it may be gone for good.

In his writings, author and leadership coach John Wooden had quite
a bit to say about character. According to him, "The true test of a man's
character is what he does when no one is watching." In other words, what
you do when you're alone reveals your true heart.

Integrity means sticking with your own ethical principles and moral
code. You may have seen news stories of men or women who committed

heroic acts in order to save someone's life. When interviewed, the heroes often remark that they were simply doing the right thing. They're talking about integrity.

In a lifetime, people have many opportunities to choose between integrity and money. The choice can be something as simple as whether to keep the extra change when the cashier accidentally hands you too much back. Or it can be complicated: how do you decide whether to take a high-paying job that could compromise your beliefs? Be a hero! Make the decision once and for all to do the right thing in every situation. Decide now to always choose your integrity over money. Trust me – you won't regret it.

Final Thoughts

Dear Nazeefah and Nabeel,

It can be difficult to think about the future. As the beauty of youth radiates from your faces, you probably can't even imagine yourselves with wrinkled skin or gray hair. But the day will come when you realize that you are no longer young and that most of your life has already happened. And when this time comes, it is my heart's desire that you accept it with grace, and with the ability to look back and know that you have lived a life of integrity and excellent character. But the only way you can look back and see this is to live it now.

Keep this advice in mind as you face your future.

All my love,
Dad

6

LET FREEDOM BE YOUR GOAL

The goal is not more money. The goal is living life on
your terms.

— CHRIS BROGAN

Confession #4

*At a young age my children thought that there was a correlation between money,
happiness and freedom. They based this perception on what they saw on television
and movies and conversations they overheard at home. For a large part of their
young lives they did not know any different and I did not help with this warped
perception.*

In the *Brower Quadrant*, author Lee Brower says, "We have true wealth
when we enjoy financial abundance without neglecting our relationships,
our communities, or our personal search for meaning." But it turns out
that this is more easily said than done. It is important to find a balance
between our money and our life purpose. Brower refers to these two categories as our financial and experience assets.

Financial assets consist of all material belongings, money, real estate, retirement plans, investments, and businesses. Conversely, experience assets encompass the abundance of knowledge, joy, and fulfillment acquired during a well-lived life. Your experience assets may involve education, travel, reputation, and traditions.

A life absorbed by financial assets could lack significance, but financial resources can provide the freedom to engage in desired life experiences. It is common for people to want money just for the sake of having it. If you ask these people why they want money, they may shrug their shoulders and say something vague as, "I just do. If I had money, I could do whatever I want to do." They instinctively realize that money can open doors and present certain freedoms, but they don't understand how. People like this have no real goals in life and so they want money to buy things and live a life of leisure in hopes of escaping the mundane and unpleasant things in life. In other words, they think money will give them the freedom to escape life as most people know it.

But here's the problem: simply having money doesn't resolve all of our difficulties. Each day, we still must face life's challenges and difficulties and decide how to respond. Money isn't simply a cure-all for life's challenges.

People become successful in life when they realize that money can serve as a tool, providing them the freedom to act on their goals, dreams, and core beliefs. Money doesn't create these dreams in itself – but it can be a tool for facilitating them. What's important is learning to recognize the difference.

Final Thoughts

Dear Nazeefah and Nabeel,

It is my hope that you will realize at a young age that having money is not for the purpose of inflating your ego, acquiring friends, or exalting yourself. As I have said before and will say many times again, money is a tool that we have passed on to you so that you may carry out your life's purpose and define your personal freedom. I want money to be a tool that brings you freedom of choice — not a heavy burden that weighs you down. Freedom, not money, buys happiness.

Yours,

Dad

7

SOME RICH PEOPLE LIVE POOR LIVES

Money won't create success, the freedom to make it will.

— Nelson Mandela

Confession #5

My kids thought that what they wore and whom they associated with was a reflection of who they were. They failed to understand that having a myopic and materialistic outlook on life was far more destructive and debilitating than not having wealth.

Early in life, we learn that to be socially accepted, we must present ourselves in certain ways. Some individuals focus on outward appearances, striving for money. These people believe that material wealth and physical appearances will help earn them acceptance and recognition.

This behavior can be seen in today's market for knockoffs of designer merchandise: may people want to give the appearance of wealth, even if they can't afford the material possessions they want. To them, the item is not as important as creating the appearance of wealth in itself. A well-made leather purse manufactured by a good company can be attractive, carry your baggage, and last many years if taken care of. A well-made leather purse without a designer label costs hundreds of dollars less than one with a designer label. And yet people still choose to pay extra for the designer purse, simply because its logo shouts, "This is a very expensive purse and I have the means to buy it."

No matter how much money one spends, having the perfect appearance becomes a never-ending competition that never ends. Due to their poor attitude about wealth, those who enter this race will never know the satisfaction of money well spent or a life well lived.

People who have good character and a rich life are secure in their identity and self worth, regardless of their financial worth. These individuals know what they want in life, and are smart enough to know that while money may provide a certain degree of freedom, it is not a final goal to strive for.

When people live rich lives, they consider how other people and the world around them are affected by their wealth, through the choices they make. These people do not have the mentality that everything is all about them, nor do they believe all of their financial resources should be spent for their own pleasures – these individuals generally tend to put some of their money towards good use and benefit of others.

Real life is composed of family, relationships, meaningful work, and worthwhile endeavors. Someone who does not understand financial wealth may obsess about money – day and night – often at the expense of the rest of their lives. These individuals worry that someone will take their money from them, or that they will make a critical mistake that could suddenly empty their bank accounts. Life passes them by while they live in fear about losing the money that should be serving them rather than the other way around. Ebenezer Scrooge is a good example of a rich person with a poor mentality.

People with a compromised mentality think that one of the greatest benefits of being rich is not working. They do not realize that work is as important as play. It gives one a sense of purpose and the ability to step beyond their normal comfort level. Through work, we learn. Play is not so sweet unless we have work with which to compare it. This does not mean that a wealthy person must have a job. There are many forms of quality work that exist outside of the workplace.

Final Thoughts

Dear Nazeefah and Nabeel,

Your mother and I wish for you to live rich lives. Even though we can provide you with the financial means, we know that only you can create a life that is rich with meaning on your own. Define what success means to you. Let your wealth be only a part of your rich life — not your entire life.

With the greatest hope that you will find the abundance of meaning that you deserve.

All my love,

Dad

8

THE STORY OF THE FISHERMAN

Richness is not abundance in material things, but the
abundance of the soul.

— Al Bukhari

A short story might help to elucidate the importance of having an abundance of the soul over material goods, throughout your life. An American businessman is standing at the pier of a small coastal Mexican village, when a small boat with just one fisherman docks. Inside the boat are several large yellow fin tuna. The American compliments the fisherman on the quality of his fish and asked how long it took him to catch them. The fisherman replies that it only took a short while.

The businessman asks the fisherman why he didn't stay out longer and catch more fish. The fisherman says he has enough fish to support his family's immediate needs. The businessman then asks, "But what do you do with the rest of your time?"

The fisherman replies, "I sleep late, fish a little, play with my children, take siesta with my wife, Maria, and stroll into the village each evening where I sip wine and play guitar with my amigos. I have a full and happy life."

The American businessman scoffs. "I am a Harvard MBA and could help you. You should spend more time fishing and with the proceeds buy a bigger boat. With the proceeds from the all the fish you can catch with a bigger boat, you can buy several boats. Eventually, you would have a fleet of fishing boats and bring in many times more fish. Instead of selling your catch to a middleman, you could sell directly to the processor, and eventually open your own cannery. You could control the product, processing, and distribution. Of course, you would need to leave this small coastal fishing village and move to Mexico City, then LA, and eventually New York City where you will run your expanding enterprise."

The fisherman asks, "But how long would all of this take? Would it take many years?"

The businessman replies, "Only about fifteen to twenty years."

"But what then?" the fisherman asks.

The American laughs and says, "When the time is right, you will be able to announce an IPO and sell your company stock to the public. You will become very rich. You'll make millions."

"Millions? But then what?"

The American says, "Then comes the best part of all. You will retire, move to a small coastal fishing village where you can fish a little, play with your kids, take siesta with your wife, and stroll to the village in the evenings to sip wine and play your guitar with your amigos."

Final Thoughts

Dear Nazeefah and Nabeel,
If you keep in mind what really matters in life, you may find that it is already much closer than you think. All work and no play is not the

answer — it can create an endless cycle of working to live. Slow down, reassess, and get real about how you want to live life.

With this in mind, your dreams await.

With love,

Dad

9

DO YOU NEED IT, OR DO YOU WANT IT?

Time is your friend; impulse is your enemy.

— JOHN BOGLE

Confession #6

My kids grew up understanding that everything was a necessity, no matter how small or large. They did not differentiate between their needs and wants, and lacked the patience to understand the difference. I admit it: as parents, my wife and I were responsible for this.

If your goal were mere survival, knowing the difference between a want and need would be simple. You can survive with just a few essentials – in fact, much of the world's population does this on a daily basis! People manage to lead happy lives with very few material possessions and what is necessary to live.

To survive, you really just need enough food and water to keep your body functioning. On top of this, you need some clothing and shelter, perhaps a heat source for winter, and a few other odds and ends. Really, this could all be contained in one small room. Compare this to the list of what most people in our society consider "needs." The difference is astounding!

Granted, life is about more than just surviving. In modern society, there are many things that are necessary for quality of life but are not essential to survival. This list will not be the same for all people. For instance, blind people can survive without a walking cane, but they need one in the sense that it helps keep them safe when they are walking. You may need a car in order to remain employed, as it is a part of your employment agreement for you to have reliable transportation. However, you probably don't need a brand new $300,000 sports car to get to work. A car may be a necessity in order to keep your job. However, a new sports car is beyond what's necessary to keep your job.

Life is short and you want to make the most of it; you don't want to spend your days struggling to survive. And to be fair, there's nothing wrong with wanting some things and attaining them. The problems arise when you can no longer differentiate your necessities from your desires.

Living a rich life is about so much more than your possessions. You don't want to spend your life collecting material things, but it can become a habit if you do not learn to recognize the difference between a want and a need, and learn to get what you need, but limit the wants.

In many instances, people are so used to wanting new things that they don't even stop to think about why they want them. Before you pursue something, ask yourself why you want it. You may decide that it's not really that important for you to have that item. Perhaps you thought you wanted it because your peers have it. Maybe you have a habit of buying the latest fashions or electronics just because they're new.

Unfortunately, others often determine the standard for what you "need." Bluntly put, companies decide what you need based on what they want to sell you. Advertising agents have learned that if they convince you that you need something, rather than only want it, you are apt to buy it. It's important to always keep this in mind. Advertising has trained the public to think in terms of need instead of want. Many people justify irresponsible spending with claims that they "need" something when they really only want it.

Ask yourself, "Will having this object, taking this adventure/trip, or participating in this event, or whatever the situation may be, truly change my life (or someone else's) for the better?" If it would, what would the change be? Be honest with yourself!

_____

Final Thoughts

_____

Dear Nazeefah and Nabeel,

The little burst of happiness you get from short-term choices quickly fades away. Before buying something new, ask yourself if you need it or if you simply want it. It's such a simple question, yet it can be profoundly useful when making purchasing decisions. We have tried to prepare you to understand the difference between a want and a need. Choose wisely!

Your Dad

10

WHEN IS ENOUGH REALLY ENOUGH?

> Money has never made man happy, nor will it. There is
> nothing in its nature to produce happiness. The more of
> it one has, the more one wants.
>
> — BENJAMIN FRANKLIN

Confession #7

The desire to accumulate material items has prevented my kids from understanding "when enough is really enough." Their possessions have sometimes become their priorities and they forget to master the art of living a simple and happy life.

It is human nature to never be satisfied. When we discover a food that we like, we want to eat more of it. When we discover a new hobby, we want to spend all of our time doing it, perhaps even becoming obsessed with it. How many times have you heard someone say, "Skateboarding, video games, basketball, making jewelry, hiking, traveling, cooking, reading, swimming...is my life!"

Some people even say, "*Shopping* is my life." When I venture into the crowded malls, I certainly have seen this to be true for some shoppers. I especially believe it if I am in a hurry to buy what I need and get out of the mall—as is often the case with dads! When people say that something is their life, they are saying that they love doing that thing and are, in a sense, literally exchanging their life for it – life is made up of time, after all.

So, how do you know when you have crossed the line and ventured into shopping obsession? It is not like you have a shopping meter that tells you when enough is enough. Your parents may tell you that you have reached that point, but as with so many things, parents may have a tendency to say this before you are ready to hear it.

And so, it's up to you to ask yourself when enough really *is* enough. The answer varies from person to person. While there is nothing wrong with having the things you want, it is important to find a balance between self-discipline and the pursuit of material goods. Asking yourself the following questions may help you reach conclusions about how much is enough.

What am I willing to do to acquire it?

Are you willing to sacrifice other parts of your life? Perhaps you are so intent on amassing things that you spend all of your time working to buy them, and have no time for family or friends as a result. You might lack time to study, be social, or make the decisions you need to make in order to move forward in your life.

Am I willing to sacrifice my future plans?

Having to downgrade or forsake future plans can happen when you make commitments for the future based on something that you want now. Young people who set their sights on an expensive car, for example, may hastily sign a lease that includes hefty monthly car payments. In turn, this may create a situation where they cannot afford to go to university without working at a job during the school year in order to make their car payment. That may affect their grades and the quality of their education.

It's certainly not just young people that make decisions to buy now and pay later. Middle-aged and older people may squander their retirement funds prematurely, simply because they want more now. The consequences, however, are serious.

Will I own it or will it own me?

Many things in life are worth investing in. It's up to you to determine when the expense is worth it. There's an old saying that goes, "own your investments, rent your fun." Do you own things that were once prized possessions, only to have found that the fun and novelty wore off quickly? If you buy something, will you still want it a month from now, or will it have become a high-maintenance chain around your neck?

Who can I talk to?

When you are acquiring things and making long-term investments and commitments, it is good to have trustworthy, experienced people to talk to – the key word being *experienced*. This may eliminate using your friends as a sounding board for important decisions on a certain topic. You may want to talk to your parents, an accountant, school counselor or personal counselor, or a personal life coach.

Am I being impatient?

Sometimes, our biggest mistakes are made when we are being impatient. When you don't know how much is enough, force yourself to take a step back. Remember to look beyond your immediate wants and ask yourself how these things fit into the bigger picture.

Am I behaving like the people that I most respect?

Look at the people in your life that you respect and admire. Do they approach life with reckless and flippant spending, gathering more and more stuff? Or do they make careful purchases, selected to fit their lifestyles?

Has obtaining possessions become my main priority?

It may sound dull and repetitive, but a life with acquiring "stuff" as the main priority is a shallow life. When one lives this kind of existence, he or she can easily lose enthusiasm, hope, and direction. That person may wander aimlessly, only to realize too late that his or her best years have been squandered.

Final Thoughts

Dear Nazeefah and Nabeel,

It is a rare person who can find the right middle ground on the spectrum between being too fearful to spend money when necessary and having an insatiable desire to spend, spend, and spend. It seems that the financial woes of many people are based on the fact that they gravitate toward one of these two extremes. At the very least, pause and give thought to where you lie on this spectrum so that you can adjust accordingly.
Dad

11

PRACTICE PATIENCE AND DELAYED GRATIFICATION

Genius is nothing but a great capacity for patience.

—Georges-Louis Leclerc Buffon

Confession #8

My children have yet to master the art of patience. How can everything be so urgent? I have been trying to help them see that living a life of patience lets us make wise decisions – and this can yield steady progress in both finances and their personal lives.

Life demands a great deal of patience if one is to live responsibly and minimize stress. For many of us however, this is easier said than done. We want what we want – and we want it now! When children are young, they are often given advice from their elders, with their tales of how things were in the "good old days." Many of these stories show how much less convenient life used to be – the point being that much patience was required in those days.

In the modern world, people feel justified in being impatient. We hate waiting for anything. Have you ever noticed the steam coming out of someone's ears in line at the coffee shop because they must wait a few minutes to order coffee? How many times have you seen people walk away in a huff because they did not receive service fast enough?

We get upset when we are delayed ten or fifteen minutes by traffic, but consider how many days (yes, days!) a 200-kilometer trip would have taken our great-great grandparents by horse and buggy. We become frustrated when our cell phones don't instantly connect to a network. We threaten to throw our laptops into the garbage when a web page is slow to load.

Our financial behaviors often demonstrate this same level of impatience. If we look back as recently as 2006, we can see that when interest rates were low, people did not save for their frivolous purchases but mortgaged and cashed out their homes to subsidize luxury vacations, high-end toys, and other goodies that they really couldn't afford. Unfortunately, when this party ended the bills came due, family homes were lost.

Patience goes hand in hand with self-discipline. To live a disciplined life, you must first learn to be patient. Patience does not come naturally for most people – it is a learned trait and must be practiced. History is full of the follies of impatience, but when people practice patience, many societal ills are eradicated.

While young people may think that patience is synonymous with *b-o-r-i-n-g*, it can also mean being able to sleep at night, free of the fallout from making impatient choices.

In most cases, we already have more than we need. Clearly, we won't suffer if we choose to put some purchases on hold until we can afford them. And once we can, the item truly belongs to us, not a bank, where we might otherwise have taken out a loan to be able to afford the purchase.. We are rewarded with a sense of accomplishment for having made the purchase without outside assistance.

Final Thoughts

Dear Nabeel and Nazeefah,
*   Patience will serve you well in all areas of your life. Like so many other important things in life, patience is something you must choose to develop for yourself. Nabeel, I was so proud of you when you patiently saved for your first iPad in 2010. You sacrificed birthday gifts, saved*

your allowance, and shoveled the driveway for extra money to buy it. You demonstrated patience, and when you got it the iPad meant much more to you.

Thoughtfully,

Dad

12

BE HONEST ABOUT MONEY

The chief cause of failure and unhappiness is trading
what you want most for what you want now.

— Zig Ziglar

Confession #9

*Even though my kids don't have jobs, they behave as if they do. They forget how little
money they have and make decisions based on their parents' income. Choices about what
kind of TV to buy or what kind of car we should drive are some of the decisions they
feel they are in the position to make.*

As one grows into an adult, he or she must become realistic about how
much money is available, what money can do, and what place it holds in
your life.

Television often provides a skewed picture of how money works.
Commercial after commercial shows people having the time of their lives,
frolicking on tropical islands, strolling through the mall with more shopping bags than they can carry. Sure – this makes for great TV, but it doesn't
show the true story. Commercials ignore the reality that consumers must

take responsibility for all of those purchases by paying for them – not to mention taking care of them and storing them.

Have you ever noticed on sitcoms that people who live in premium living quarters, travel, play lots of golf, shop, eat in fine restaurants, wear designer clothes, and drive expensive cars never seem to go to work? The new generation that was brought up on a diet of the "*Friends* phenomenon" became easily accustomed to the idea that this type of lifestyle is normal. Normal for whom, though? It would be unlikely for even someone who carefully manages his or her money to live in a major metropolitan city in a nice, large apartment and get by on a coffee shop employee's wage. Yet how many TV shows portray people living large, all the while working at a coffee shop?

Most people are not thrilled about setting a budget and living within it. Budgets clearly spell out "You can't afford that right now!" in black and white. There is no arguing when the numbers are on paper. Sticking to a budget keeps spending in check. It helps you walk on level financial ground without too many difficulties.

Final Thoughts

Dear Nazeefah and Nabeel,

It is easy to get lost in the hustle and bustle of life, losing sight of what's important where money is concerned. This makes it necessary to pause from time to time and take an honest look at your financial situation, adjusting as needed. This is every bit as true for those not facing current financial strife as it is for those struggling to make ends meet. Nazeefah, when you moved away to study, you were forced to grow up quickly. You learned how to budget, and became honest about money. How to spend, when to spend, and what to spend became your new reality.

Always here for consultation.

Dad

13

DO YOU KNOW HOW FORTUNATE YOU ARE?

It's not your salary that makes you rich. It's your spending
habits.

— CHARLES A JAFFE

Confession #10

*My kids sometimes lament that other children are more fortunate than themselves.
They fail to see how much they have and how little is expected in return. They are very
fortunate.*

According to the Human Development Report, three billion people
live on less than $2.50 per day, and about 80 percent of humans live on less
than $10 a day. The fact that you most likely can't even fathom living on
these amounts says a great deal about where you rank in the world. People
who have plenty spend more than $2.50 per day on one cup of coffee. In
fact, many people buy several cups of coffee, every day – all without a moment's hesitation about what they spend for it. Can you imagine having to
feed several children with $2.50 per day? Can you imagine having shelter,
food, and the other necessities of life if you were forced to live on $2.50
per day?

Even in developed countries, most people do not come from wealthy families; the middle class can meet all of their needs by working, but most people do not even fit into the middle class category.

Far too many children are born into poverty. These children know the reality of lacking the very basics of enough food to eat, appropriate clothing for weather conditions, and suitable, long-term shelter. While they should be able to enjoy being a carefree kid, they are faced with real problems such as the potential that their family could be evicted from their home, teasing at school for circumstances that they have no control over, and parents who are constantly stressed about finances. Crime, substance abuse, and lack of parental supervision often accompany poverty, further adding to these children's woes.

If you have never known poverty and lack for what you need, you might not understand what some people have to go through. You should understand that wealth is not owed to you. You are not entitled to wealth. You were not born with a note attached to your soft baby skin that said, "This baby is owed wealth. He/she is entitled to live a life of abundance."

You are special because you are you. Having wealth does not make you a special person, but it does give you the opportunity to do special things for yourself and others. Understanding how fortunate you are should help you realize that you do not have the same limitations as many others do. Having wealth gives you the opportunity to do what you want to do, with fewer barriers to overcome. Realizing the value of your good fortune will help you have compassion and mercy toward those who are less fortunate.

While addressing college graduates and giving them advice, billionaire Bill Gates shared advice that his mother gave to his wife, Melinda: "To whom much is given, much is expected." When a good person possesses wealth, it can lend them a certain amount of authority, which can be used to accomplish great things. Develop the habit of looking for opportunities to accomplish good things.

Final Thoughts

Dear Nazeefah and Nabeel,

When children are born to wealthy parents, it is said that they are born with a silver spoon in their mouth. I don't know about a silver spoon, but I do know that both of you were born children, primarily because you were born to parents who love you and want only the best for you. Second, you were born to parents who have the means to share wealth with you. Third, you were born to parents who want to make sure that you understand how to use that wealth for your benefit and not your detriment.

With love,

Dad

14

ARE YOU FRUGAL OR A CHEAPO?

Don't tell me where your priorities are. Show me where
you spend your money, and I'll tell you what they are.

— JAMES W. FRIC

Confession #11

My kids have not learned the difference between being cheap and living a frugal life.
Frugality has an unnecessarily bad rap. Frugality does not mean you are cheap or poor.
On the contrary, it shows strong character. It is nothing to be embarrassed about.

Frugal people realize that their lives can be complete without having every possession that they want. They are content to find happiness, peace, and joy in other ways besides gaining possessions. They consciously spend time with other people talking, exchanging ideas, and listening.

Frugality isn't just about what you buy. It's also about the way you use things. It's about conserving water by only using what you need and conserving electricity by turning off lights and electronics when not in use. It's about walking to the store or farmers' market for groceries instead of driving a car and using gasoline. People who are frugal realize that it is not considerate to waste resources that future generations may depend on.

Would you be surprised to learn that many billionaires are frugal people? They realize that the value of money lies in what you can accomplish with it. Even though they have plenty of money that allows them to do as they please, they may see no value in having the lavish material possessions often seen as must-haves for the extraordinarily wealthy.

According to Investopedia, ("6 Spending Tips from Frugal Billionaires, 2010") billionaire Warren Buffet still lives in the modest five-bedroom house that he purchased for $31,500 in 1957. From media reports, it is a well-known fact that Buffet is frugal. Does this make him cheap?

No one, not even Warren Buffet, wants to be known as a cheapskate. No one wants to be the only friend in the group who doesn't bring gifts to the host or hostess of a party, or that person known for "forgetting their wallet" in order to get their meal paid for by their friends.

Being frugal and being cheap are two very different things. Sometimes a frugal person can appear cheap and a cheap person can seem frugal. Sometimes there is a thin line between being frugal and being cheap. It seems safe to say that frugality lands somewhere between being a spendthrift and being a cheapskate. With the economic downturn in 2008, many spendthrifts quickly learned to become frugal but did not become cheapskates.

Frugal Fran vs. Chris Cheapo

Frugal Fran and Chris Cheapo are two individuals who were hit particularly hard by the financial crisis. While Fran had a couple of tough years, she eventually adapted to her changed circumstances and resumed living a full life despite her reduced means. Chris, on the other hand, became bitter and retreated into a shell, cutting himself off from the world in the process. He still refuses to spend money on anything unless he absolutely has to, treating every merchant as if they're out to get him.

Fran and Chris have both decided that they want to take advantage of their city's remarkable bicycle infrastructure to save money by riding a bike to work. But when they went shopping for their bikes, their behavior and motivations were strikingly different.

Chris was motivated entirely by money. He wanted the cheapest bike he could get and was shocked to find out how expensive even the lowest quality bikes were. He concluded that the whole industry is a scam designed to rob people of their hard-earned money. He suspected that backroom deals and kickbacks were driving up the prices, forgetting that companies incur many expenses in bringing a product to market, and that there are a lot of people who have to make a living off of these bikes. Begrudgingly, Chris forked over $100 to the local mega discount store for a steel mountain bike that was made in China and assembled by a minimum-wage worker in the back of the store.

Fran's approach could not be more different. She shopped around on-line before going out to buy, reading reviews to find out what other people think about the bikes. She also read the bicycling forums to get information from experienced bicyclists, who have much to say about quality, price, and riding style. When she made her decision, she went to a specialty bike store and spent $1,000 on a quality aluminum road bike, understanding that her investment would replace a car that costs her almost $8,000 dollars per year to operate. There are cheaper bikes available from less expensive stores, but her research informed her of the quality of the bikes at this store, so she decided that a better bike was a higher value. Besides, this store, which she ended up buying from, had a good reputation, and they offered a two-year service warranty so that she could keep her purchase in good condition.

Over the next month, Chris's and Fran's results have differed sharply. After two weeks of riding to work, Chris still hadn't adjusted to riding his bike. He would arrive at work sweaty and gasping for air, developing a reputation as "that weird bike guy." In addition, his knees and back began hurting all the time, and he had to take time off work to recover. One day, on his way home from work, Chris hit a pothole at speed and the cheap Chinese steel frame folded like a wire hanger. He tried to straighten the frame out with a rubber mallet, but the bike was ruined. Chris Cheapo now concludes that bicycling is for losers and has gone back to driving his car. In total, Chris has lost $100 on his bike and $600 in missed workdays.

Fran's new bike rides like a dream and she arrives at work every morning feeling energized and ready for action. Many of her coworkers are inspired by her new lifestyle. Soon, they take up biking themselves, often joining in on morning rides. Fran's health has improved from the exercise, and she quickly found herself in the best shape of her life, simply from her morning commute. Once she committed fully to the biking lifestyle, Fran sold her car, which will save her $32,000 over the next four years, tremendously improving her financial situation. It won't take her long to save up enough money to put a down payment on a small house in a great neighborhood. She continues to bike to work every day, and with regular maintenance, her $1,000 bike will last her a lifetime.

Fran and Chris come from similar backgrounds, but their attitudes toward life vary immensely. During the financial crisis of 2008, Chris took his losses personally and his self-esteem was damaged. He adopted a defeatist attitude, reducing his ability to function in the world and causing his relationships with other people to suffer.

Fran had a more realistic perspective on the situation. She suffered as much as anyone else at first, but she knew that she wasn't alone in this, and understood what she had to do to adapt. Her expenses had to come down, but she maintained her standards and wasn't about to allow hardship to break her, so she chose to live happily anyway.

In day-to-day life:

- ❖ Frugal Fran is cautious about her spending, seeking out value in everything she purchases. She weighs price against the value the purchase will bring to her life.
- ❖ Chris Cheapo is stingy; he looks for the lowest price on everything. Quality doesn't even enter into the decision.
- ❖ Fran looks for ways to cut her spending, and gets things done anyway. Over the past year, she has learned to do home repairs and maintain her possessions. She pays an expert when she can't do it herself, refusing to allow things to fall apart. In addition, she learned to cook her own meals so that she could eat healthy and cheap every day.

❖ Chris lets things run into the ground because he's unwilling to pay someone or learn to do things himself. As a result, his home is crumbling and none of his things work the way they are supposed to. He can't cook, and lives off of canned beans and dollar-menu hamburgers.

❖ Fran invests a small portion of her earnings on continuing education every year, and her employer reimburses her for a portion of that. As a result, she contributes knowledge capital to her company, and her income increases regularly.

❖ Chris refuses to spend any money on his education. As a result, his skills are lacking. He has fallen behind most of his coworkers, and even the new people who enter the company are more up to date than he is. His head is constantly on the chopping block. The constant risk of losing his job stresses him out.

❖ Fran spends a small amount of money each month to maintain a sensible wardrobe, replacing her clothes as they wear out or become tarnished. When she shops for clothes, she looks for the highest quality she can find, opting for good fit, sturdy materials, and skilled workmanship. Fran always looks great. She gets compliments wherever she goes.

❖ Chris never buys clothes until he absolutely has to, looking sloppy and often wearing the same outfits multiple days in a row. When he buys clothes, he buys the cheapest he can find, which often fit poorly and wear out quickly. He wears his poor attitude. Unsurprisingly, people avoid him like the plague.

❖ Fran goes out with her friends from time to time, spending a sensible amount of money to nourish her relationships with others. She is involved in her community and always has something to do.

❖ Chris never goes anywhere or does anything except work. Most of his free time is spent on the couch in front of the television, where his life is wasted and his mind turns to mush. His few friends are just like him, When they do get together, it's for pizza in front of the TV.

❖ Fran has health insurance. She visits the doctor regularly for checkups, knowing that people in her family have had health issues in

CONFESSIONS OF A DAD 51

the past. She's confident that her diligence will help her catch medical problems before they become serious.

❖ Chris doesn't have health insurance. He avoids going to the doctor until his seemingly constant illnesses become a serious threat to his life.

❖ Fran is engaged to someone who really cares about her, and they're getting married soon. They will have a reasonable wedding with their families and close friends, enjoying the moment with their loved ones.

❖ Chris used to be engaged, but his fiancée dumped him a long time ago when he let his life fall into ruins. He wants a girlfriend, but his self-esteem is so bad due his lifestyle that he's afraid to talk to women.

❖ Fran gives to charity every year, and helps out those who need aid from time to time. She writes off her charitable contributions on her taxes to increase her refund.

❖ Chris never gives a cent to charity, and never has any spare change for the beggar's cup.

Chris and Fran were both respectable people. Fran adapted to the changing economic climate and became wiser for it, learning the value of the dollar and the importance of squeezing as much as possible from life. Chris did not adapt but instead became a shadow of his former self. His bad attitude and lack of financial wisdom has driven him into a difficult position.

Final Thoughts

Dear Nazeefah and Nabeel,
    It has been one of my goals to be frugal. While I have often been met with accusations of being cheap (in a friendly way, of course!), I have tried to teach the value of frugality to you. There is a difference

between being cheap and being frugal. The tale of Chris Cheapo may be a sad one, but it is the fate of many that are afflicted with financial hardship. They take it personally, develop a poor attitude, and slowly fall into poverty. Those like Frugal Fran, who have the ability to retain their clear thinking in the face of challenges, can survive lean times, and even become better people for it.

Keep this is mind as you pursue your financial decisions for the future.

With love,

Dad

15

FINANCIAL COMFORT ZONE

Two things define you. Your patience when you have
nothing, and your attitude when you have everything.

— UNKNOWN

Confession #12

I must admit that the words "financial emergency" are not part of my kids' vo-
cabulary. To them, a financial emergency means not having money to buy the most
expensive prom dress or a brand name winter jacket. They fail to understand that
if they do not plan for actual life emergencies, their lives can become desperate with
very little warning.

When you work at a job for a few years and get comfortable with its
routine and benefits, it's easy to settle in and become complacent.

But when you wake up to your financial situation, pay down debt,
and establish new routines that aren't as costly, you begin to simply enjoy
the lower bills and freedom to make choices – let alone protect yourself
against potential financial surprises.

Settling in is the easy thing to do. It's the path of least resistance – so
unless you consciously make other choices, it's conceivable that you'll wind

up following that path, too. The problem is that settling in is more dangerous than you might expect. Settling in assumes that what comes easy today will last forever.

If you're coasting in your career, you might not recognize opportunities for a great promotion at work, or a new job opportunity that could put you in a great place. You're also making the dangerous assumption that your current job is secure.

If you're coasting with your finances, you're making the assumption that your income will remain stable and you'll just eventually take care of all of your debts and your goals. You might not be prepared to take advantage of something when it comes along. You'll never see the changes in your life coming.

The challenge for all of us is to avoid falling into a comfort zone. But when such comfort zones are so easy to fall into, how can we avoid them?

How can we keep ourselves ready for change when there doesn't seem to be any change on the horizon?

Here are a few ways to consider.

Prepare for change as part of your day-to-day routine.

Part of your professional routine should be to keep your résumé fresh by pursuing educational opportunities and taking on professional challenges within the workplace. You should be improving your financial state on a monthly basis, constantly seeking out new ways to ramp up the improvement.

Start a to do list.

Start a list of items on your agenda. Add to it whenever you find something that you could do to beef up your financial security. We all have great ideas that we lose from time to time because we didn't take a moment to write them down before forgetting them.

Spend some time each week to examine the various areas of your life.

Ask yourself what you're doing to improve yourself in terms of finances, hobbies, community, academic aspirations, and anything else that you're involved with. If there's something you can identify that you're not doing right now to actively improve, take a moment and add it to your to-do list.

Envision disaster scenarios.

What exactly would happen in your life if you were to lose your job? What if you fell ill? What about your parents? What about you?

Walk yourself through these scenarios a little bit. What would you do? Next, choose some steps that you could take, right now, to make that scenario go smoother if it ever should occur. Add those steps to your to-do list.

The key to these steps is to do things that will make you better prepared for opportunities and disasters. Riding in the comfort zone leaves you complacent and poorly prepared. Every day, you have the opportunity to make yourself ready for whatever might come your way.

Final Thoughts

Dear Nazeefah and Nabeel,

I must warn you about the pitfalls of being complacent. Allow yourselves to be comfortable in this life, but be aware of financial danger. Have a level of alertness that allows you to detect opportunities and disasters and to have a plan of action to adequately deal with any emergency that may arise.

Love,
Dad

PART TWO: MONEY HABITS AND STRATEGIES

Your net worth to the world is usually determined by what remains after your bad habits are subtracted from your good ones.

— BENJAMIN FRANKLIN

16

INSANITY

The definition of insanity is remaining in debt year after
year and continuing to use your credit cards.

— AZHAR LAHER

Confession #13

*I am amazed at how many times my children have made the same financial mistakes
over and over again. Insanity aside, they fail to realize that if they don't change their
behavior, they can't expect to get different results.*

I have recited Einstein's definition of insanity to my kids so many
times that they now finish the sentence for me. I use the statement often
because it stops me from making the same mistakes again and again, and
in the hope that my kids will learn a life lesson.

How can people expect to lose weight when they keep eating the same
diet that caused them to gain weight in the first place?

How can anyone expect to get rich when they stick to the same work
routines and spending habits that have inhibited them?

This statement is merely a call to change; if you want to achieve different
results, you must first change your behavior.

Many people find it difficult to stay on a path to financial freedom and to consistently make financially responsible decisions. Most positive actions will generate positive results, and will be beneficial over the long term. Even better, the more financially responsible you are, the easier it becomes.

Staying on a financially responsible path requires small steps, which will eventually lead to financial transformation in your life.

Stay for the long haul.

If everyone were suddenly able to achieve great financial health after just a few days of not using his or her credit cards, you can bet that this is exactly what most people would do. If a great body and physical health were the result of a week's worth of jogging and eating salads, people would do those things and then veg out, consuming whatever they like.

Unfortunately, life doesn't work that way.

Make permanent changes.

The hole that takes many years to dig will take a long time to fill back in. There is no magic button that will reverse the debt, the weight gain, or even the shyness you've conditioned in yourself.

That said, every single step in the right direction – however small it may be – is a positive effort toward change. But realize that you won't see permanent results in the first week, or even the first month. Instead, what you should aim for is a new path that will take you where you want to go.

It took me seven years to create my own "financial freedom" and "debt freedom." Much of this time revolved around teaching myself how to live in a new way and how to spend less than I earned. Each small change that I made was one step on the right path. It was my patience that made all the difference.

It may be insane to do the same thing over and over and expect different results, but it's also insane to change a few things and expect to see long-term, drastic results immediately. If you want change, you must the entire path that you're on, not simply behave differently for a short period.

Final Thoughts

Dear Nazeefah and Nabeel,

For years, I have been misplacing my car keys and wallet. Instead of having one place to keep these valuable possessions, I still waste time every day looking for them. As I've taught you both, this is insanity – doing the same thing over and over and expecting a different result. If you continue to spend more than you earn, the outcome will be the same until you change your habits.

Love,

Dad

17

DON'T SPEND BLINDLY

Do not save what is left after spending, but spend what is
left after saving.

— WARREN BUFFETT

Confession #14

*When it comes to spending, one of the most important habits you can develop in your
life is discipline. Unfortunately, my kids forget to "save for a rainy day" because they
have not yet formed good money habits. People who spend blindly and frivolously need
to change their habits and become disciplined. They need to see the value of repairing the
roof before it starts to rain.*

You may have heard the joke "But I can't be out of money! I still have
checks left!"

Of course, this joke was popular when people still used checks as their
main form of payment for shopping, paying bills, and so forth. Today, the
equivalent would be, "I can't be out of money! I still have a credit card!"

When you get your paycheck or allowance, or when we deposit
money into your checking account for university expenses, it must seem
like you have plenty of cash to spend. This may also be the case when

you get scholarship money or school loans. Receiving significant sums of money all at once may tempt you to go to the mall, to attend an expensive event with friends, or to purchase a pricey product that you want. If you have gone without much spending or shopping money for a while, the urge can be especially strong. It's easy to rationalize that you deserve to have some fun or to go shopping, and that you'll worry about the details later.

You may spend without keeping track of your money, and before you realize it, you have accidentally spent more than you had available to spend, even though there is still money in your account. You may have exceeded your spending limit and used funds meant for bills, expenses, or your savings account. Suddenly, you're "in the red" even though you just got paid.

That sinking feeling might churn in your gut, as you wonder why you bought things that you really didn't plan on buying. You might become stressed and contemplate if you will cover your expenses.

Before Nazeefah left home for university, she had never been in complete control of her own finances. This was all about to change. We agreed that she would be responsible for managing her own finances and sticking to a budget. She had been at school for a few weeks before she checked her bank account. Her account reflected the money we had deposited for the semester.

I helped create a budget with her and we spoke several times over the previous summer about how to manage her school expenses and personal expenses. I remember when she called me and said that she had a lot of money in her account and I immediately reminded her that the money should last for the duration of the semester. She was disappointed that she could not go out and purchase stuff at the mall! After all, she had money in her account.

In the second semester, I was surprised to see that she had spent most of the money in her account on "personal items" rather than setting aside money to purchase her textbooks. To her credit, she realized that she had made a mistake. She immediately made plans to earn additional income by finding a part-time job. Sometimes, the best learning happens after you realize the error of your ways. Find the silver lining in every bad situation.

The best way to avoid this type of scenario is to plan before you spend—always. Never blindly spend your money simply because there is still cash in your account. You should determine where your funds will be allocated before you start spending. Look at your written budget and determine the amount of money you will need to cover tuition expenses and personal expenses. After planning on paper, you can determine what you can freely spend, and then decide how you really want to spend it.

Final Thoughts

Dear Nazeefah and Nabeel,

I get it—it's fun to spend with reckless abandon. Who doesn't want to feel like a kid with a credit card? But as young adults, discipline and prudence must be exercised in spending. I know you understand, so always plan before you spend. Save the excitement of using your credit card for when you're in the position to immediately pay it off.

Love,
Dad

18

HABITS MATTER! THE STORY OF BABY ELEPHANTS

Generosity is giving more than you can, and pride is taking less than you need.

— KAHLIL GIBRAN

"Practice makes perfect," the old saying goes. When someone repeats
the same behavior – whether good or bad – the behavior becomes a
habit.

When trainers work with baby elephants to prepare them for their
life of performance, they tether the elephant to a stake in the ground
and it is free to walk the length of the tether. The elephant quickly becomes accustomed to the tether and the boundaries that it creates. It
becomes the habit of the young elephant to walk the circumference day
after day.

As the elephant develops the habit of walking the circumference, the
trainer removes the tether. Once it is free of its constraints, the habit of
walking the circle created by the length of the tether is so ingrained in the
elephant that it continues to go to that spot and walk the circumference

even when the tether is gone. That's what the elephant has been conditioned to do.

And so it is when you develop good money habits of your own! If you learn these behaviors when you are young, they will stay with you for the rest of your life. Developing the habit of carrying out your financial plans will allow them to progress beyond just being plans.

Create a good plan and develop good personal and financial habits that will ensure that you will carry it out. If you plan to save money for your retirement, develop the habit of putting a percentage of every paycheck into a retirement account. If you plan to start your own business, develop the habit of studying business periodicals, attending business seminars, enrolling in business classes, and spending time with business owners who can answer questions and share what their experiences and lessons learned.

We might think that our lives are shaped by the defining moments, but in reality, our daily routines make us who we are. Habits matter!

Here are some tips to get you started with good money habits.

Keep learning about personal finance.

Never assume that you already know everything there is to know about money and wealth. You can always learn more.

Create a savings strategy, and continue to save.

Determine exactly how much of your paycheck you will need to save and how much you can afford to spend. Even when you would prefer to do something else with your money, be disciplined and put at least a portion of your earnings into savings.

Always remember that you are the master of your money.

Keep in mind that you are the master of your money; it is not the master of you.

Remember that money does not determine your character, integrity, or core belief system.

Money cannot take the place of the internal moral in your life.

Remain thankful for what you have and protect your finances.

Do not be careless with your money. Realize that you have the responsibility to preserve the wealth that has been passed down to you.

Always live within your means.

Do not spend more than you have available to spend. Be especially aware of not living outside of your budget in order to impress others.

Final Thoughts

Dear Nazeefah and Nabeel,

They say that good habits only take twenty-one days to form. If you develop good money habits, along with an expectation for possibility and opportunity in your life, that is what you will find. High expectations combined with an effort to develop positive habits, discipline, and hard work, is a formula for success in any area of life.

I hope to help you instill the habits now that will ensure a lifetime of success.

With high hopes for your future,
Dad

19

BEWARE OF THE DIDEROT EFFECT

Do not spoil what you have by desiring what you have
not; but remember that what you now have was once
among the things you only hoped for.

— EPICURUS, GREEK PHILOSOPHER

Confession #15

My kids insist on upgrading their existing gadgets, even though they are in perfect working order. Smaller and faster seems to be the new normal.

Because possessions appear to be the new metric for success, people spend a good deal of their time accumulating "stuff." You may think that only the wealthy do this since they are the ones who have access to immense funds. But the desire to prove your self-worth and find happiness in things is just as rampant among those without wealth, and even among the poor.

The more stuff a person collects, the more time he or she must devote to take care of it. If one is not careful, he or she can spend an entire life, one day at a time, earning money to get stuff, buy stuff, and take care of the stuff they buy. Here is a story to illustrate my point.

In the eighteenth century, the French writer Denis Diderot received an extravagant gift far beyond anything he could have afforded to purchase. It was a beautiful scarlet dressing gown made with luxurious fabric fit for royalty. The rich color and superb artisanship of the robe caught the attention of everyone.

Upon receiving the beautiful robe, Diderot threw away his well-worn and plain, but practical, old robe. He decided he did not need it any longer. In fact, he believed himself to be above wearing such plain robes when he could wear one of much higher quality. Of course, wearing the new robe meant that Diderot had to make a few changes and buy a few more things.

When he had worn his old robe, the writer had simply used the sleeve as a duster when one of his books became dusty. Now, he clearly could not wipe away dust with his fine new gown sleeve, so he needed to buy some dusting rags.

When he had worn his old robe, he used the hem to wipe away excess ink on his pen. He could not do that with his new garment, so he needed to buy handkerchiefs to do the job. Better yet, he would buy new pens that work better and not leave so much excess ink. It would be a small amount to spend in order to preserve his beautiful new robe.

In comparison to his new robe, Diderot noticed that the rest of the belongings in his humble home looked shabby. The drapes were old and faded, for he'd had them for many years. He was no longer content with them and knew they would have to be replaced. So, he bought heavy drapes of fine velvet to cover the windows.

The old straw chair that he sat on when he worked would no longer suffice. Diderot was afraid he would snag the fabric of his robe on the straw. Besides, he looked like royalty with the robe on and it looked silly for such a royal-looking man to sit on a cheap straw chair. He replaced the straw chair with one made of fine Moroccan leather, in a shade that complimented his scarlet gown. Thinking that he would be happy and feel great sitting in the new chair and wearing the new robe, Diderot sat down at his desk to work. As soon as he sat down, he encountered another problem. The rickety old desk he had used for so long seemed very much out of place among the elegant drapes and expensively adorned chair. So, he purchased a handsome desk with ornate carved legs and covered it in fine scarlet fabric.

Again, he sat down to work, expecting that with his fine surroundings and expensive desk, he would create his very best writing. He felt he would now write masterpieces! But alas, as he looked over the desk at the wall, the simple paintings looked amateurish, with the colors dull and faded. He knew he would have to replace the paintings with exquisite art from a known artist.

Counting his money, Diderot knew that he had spent more on furnishing his writing studio than he had allotted for living for the next year. He knew that it would be unwise to spend even more and that purchasing the things he truly needed over the next year would cause him to go into debt. Nonetheless, he could not stop his spending. He had created the image of finery in his mind and he was determined to complete it. He rubbed the only two gold coins that remained in his wallet and thought about how his friends and other writers would envy him for his purchases. Smiling, he thought about how they would esteem him because he looked to be a wealthy writer, even though he would truly be penniless and in debt if he purchased artwork.

Diderot purchased new paintings for his wall. He put on his fancy robe and sat in his Moroccan leather chair situated behind his ornately carved desk. From his desk, he admired the drapes that covered the window and the paintings that adorned the wall. Now, at last, he was ready to write.

The author picked up his new pen and dipped it in ink, anticipating the flow of eloquent and extraordinary prose on the blank page before him. But the words did not come. For days, the words did not come.

He had been so busy buying "one more thing" to look like a successful writer that he had not thought of his writing at all for several weeks. He found that his mind was filled with images of rich fabric and the artifacts of luxury but not a single profound phrase or thought. He tried to listen his heart to see if there were some ideas there, but he could hear nothing. His heart was filled only with the desire to buy more things.

When Diderot was finally able to find words, he penned an essay. The essay was not about how happy he was to have gained so many new possessions but rather about how his new robe had actually been a curse rather than a blessing, because it stole his mind and heart away from what he really was—a contented writer. He wrote that he had been the master of his old robe but had become enslaved to his new one.

In the twenty-first century, the things that Diderot purchased would be different, but we still see the exact same story play out in modern times. People today are masters of buying the stuff they need to achieve their desired look. If a man buys an Armani suit, he feels uncomfortable being seen in his ten-year-old car, so he goes into debt to purchase a new car that looks better with his Armani suit. That car does not look right parked in front of his modest apartment, so he buys a bigger house in a ritzier part of the city, acquiring a mortgage that requires creative budgeting each month. He has to show off his new house, so he entertains guests. The usual gathering of a few good friends at a backyard barbecue no longer satisfies him, so he throws lavish parties for his new neighbors.

Before long, the man works so many extra hours to pay for his stuff that he lacks time to enjoy life. He longs for friends who care about him for who he is, not what he has. He is tired. He wishes he had never bought the Armani suit!

Is the moral of this story to avoid buying an Armani suit? No, of course not! Instead, set your standard of living to authentically improve your life, enrich your talents, and provide what you need, but do not develop the habit of always thinking you have to buy "one more thing" to improve your life, feel better, work better, or look better.

Having a lifestyle requires discipline. Time, attention, and often money are scarce resources. The beauty of a lifestyle is that it provides guidance regarding what to do or not do in terms of what's worth having or not having.

Final Thoughts

Dear Nazeefah and Nabeel,
 The famous author Diderot had it right: If something is comfortable and it works for you, keep it. We often think that material possessions will bring lasting excitement into our life, but most of the time

they just end up getting in the way of life. Have you ever purchased something—something you really wanted—only to discover that it made the rest of your stuff seem a bit old and dated? I remember when I bought a new big screen TV for our home, only to decide that I needed a new DVD player to go with it. The old DVD player was in good working order and I was behaving irrationally. Nabeel, remember when you saved up and purchased your Mac computer? You wanted a cover to protect your new computer and so you discarded your old cover even though it was in good condition. There is a saying, "be content with very little or you will not be content with very much."

I want for you to have much, but to be content with little.

Yours,

Dad

20

THE NEW NORMAL—USING PLASTIC

A wise man should always have money in his head, but
not in his heart.

— JONATHAN SWIFT

Confession #16

Both of my children were given the responsibility of owning their credit cards at a very young age. I gave these to them as a tool for them to learn about money and credit. They were excited because they thought they had unlimited access to money. They did not understand that when they used their credit cards, they were in fact using money that belonged to the bank and that the bank was merely loaning them money (at a very high-interest rate!)

You have probably heard many warnings against obtaining and using credit cards. In some cases, such warnings are well-founded. When a person uses credit cards unwisely and without restraint, he or she can quickly create financial woes. When spending is out of control, credit cards can become an "enabler" of sorts for the spender. Out-of-control credit card spending has been the demise of many healthy financial situations.

On the other hand, a credit card can be required in many common situations, even when putting something on hold and paying cash for the actual purchase. Credit cards are usually required for making reservations for hotels and rental cars, purchasing flight tickets, or reserving event seats. Forgoing credit cards entirely is not necessarily a good idea. While many people acquire more credit card debt than they can manage, self-discipline and good money management is the solution!

Furthermore, credit cards can be used to your advantage. You can establish a positive credit history by applying for a credit card in your name and using it wisely. You might not believe it now, but there will come a time when having good credit will make a difference to your borrowing costs.

Most credit card companies offer fraud protection to allow you to shop and complete transactions with confidence. When you buy expensive items, the added consumer protection can be quite valuable. In real emergencies where large sums of money are needed instantly, a credit card can be a lifesaver. In less critical situations, having a credit card handy can save you from some embarrassing moments.

However, entering the credit card arena should be done with serious consideration. Incredibly, some people (yes, even older adults) see plastic as "extra" money at their disposal. *Credit is not money that you own: it is borrowed money.*

When you use credit cards, you are using someone else's money – and you must give it back with added interest and fees. Let that be a mantra that you repeat every time you slip your credit card out of your wallet!

No matter how much credit card companies try to convince you that they are in the business of providing you with security and the means to get the most out of life, they're really in the business of making money, and they are very good at what they do. You, on the other hand, are in the business of using your money as wisely as you can, so you have more of it to pursue your goals, help the less fortunate, and save.

That means that you need to read the fine print on credit card offers and applications very carefully. Charges, fees, and interest rates vary from one card to another, even though government regulations provide some standards and limitations. Some companies charge an annual fee just for having their card, even if you do not use it. In addition to interest (the cost of using the bank's money may differ based on different criteria of applicants) on purchases and cash withdrawals, the interest can be higher on cash withdrawals than purchases. There are also penalties for making late monthly payments and charging over your credit limit.

Your credit score, debt-to-income ratio, and credit history are the primary factors that determine credit card interest rates. If you have not established good credit or if you have a poor credit score, the interest rate on your card will be on the higher end. If you have an excellent credit score and credit history, you may be able to negotiate the lowest interest rate available. Don't be afraid to ask for a lower rate if you meet the qualifications for lower interest rates. Let the credit card company know that you are serious about managing your money, and that you want to use a company that takes your finances seriously.

To help maintain a healthy financial picture, make every payment on or before the due date each month. Even if you pay just a few days after the designated day, it can show up as a late payment on your credit record. If you are the disorganized type, try to get yourself set up so that it's easy to make on-time payments. If you cannot seem to manage that, go for a credit card that offers a grace period on late payments so you do not incur late fees.

Do your best to pay your entire balance off every month. If you find you are having a difficult time doing so, it may indicate that you should re-evaluate your spending habits.

At the very least, pay the minimum amount due on your credit card each month. Keep in mind that if you pay only the minimum each month, most of your payment will go toward interest and fees; you will not make much progress toward paying off the principal balance owed. The trap of the credit card companies is that once a person begins making only the minimum payment each month, he or she may become a customer for life!

Even mature adults can get into trouble with credit cards. Chances are, you will wisely manage your credit cards, but if you find that you are in a deeper financial hole than you realized, don't ignore the problem – it will only get worse. Talk to your parents, a trusted adult, or a financial advisor right away. The sooner you face the problem, the sooner you can work out a solution. It takes courage to swallow your pride and to admit your troubles, but in the end it will save you a large degree of stress.

Signs that you may be in trouble with your credit card include:

- ❖ You use credit cards for impulse buying.
- ❖ You don't stick to your budget, but instead use your credit card to pay for items that go over your budget.
- ❖ You don't pay off your entire balance most or all months.
- ❖ Your monthly payments are late.
- ❖ You only make the minimum payments most or all months.
- ❖ You keep the card maxed out to the limit most of the time.
- ❖ You apply for another credit card to help meet expenses because your primary card is maxed out.
- ❖ You feel stressed because of the balance on the credit card.

Final Thoughts

Dear Nazeefah and Nabeel,

Managing finances, particularly credit cards, requires discipline. Plastic may be the new normal, but trust me – you don't want to have the problems that come with mismanagement of credit cards. Use them wisely and let them work for you, rather than against you.
Dad

21

THE ONLINE SHOPPING SLOPE

Time for reflection and interaction is a casualty of the digital age, and one of the primary goals of higher education should be to reclaim this time.

— Jose Antonio Bowen

Confession #17

The Internet generation has changed the way we shop, work, and play. My children's relationship with technology has allowed them to achieve more with less. My kids are far better multitaskers than I ever was, and their ability to juggle three, four, and even five tasks at the same time is impressive. However, their ability to focus on only one conversation is less impressive.

It seems the whole world lives on the Internet. We are a plugged-in, online nation. Everywhere you go, there are people staring at their phones, tablets, and laptops. They are engaged in social media, movies, music, business, and...shopping.

Because you can find almost anything you could ever want to buy online, it can be enticing to explore and search for the perfect item. Even

if you live in a small town in the middle of nowhere, . Because online re-
tailers have fewer overheads than traditional brick-and-mortar stores, they
can offer better prices. Over all, this is a value to customers, but it can also
be part of the slippery slope of online shopping.

Online shopping is available twenty-four hours a day, seven days a
week, 365 days a year – literally! Has the convenience and constant avail-
ability of online shopping turned us into a nation of materialistic monsters?

Humor writer Erma Bombeck once said, "The odds of going to the
store for a loaf of bread and coming out with only a loaf of bread are three
billion to one." We know this to be especially true where online shopping
is concerned. Perhaps we innocently go online to look for a new pair of
comfortable shoes, but do we simply find said shoes, purchase them, and
move on? Not if online advertisers have anything to say about it! Most
likely, we will see several other items that catch our attention while we are
looking for the shoes we need – and all too often, we gladly oblige, with
credit card in hand.

For the undisciplined spender, online shopping can be as destructive
as leaving a child alone in a candy shop. While the child may end up with a
tummy ache for a few hours, the compulsive spender can end up with severe financial pain for months or years to come. All it takes is a few clicks
to spend boatloads of money online. And many websites keep credit card
information on file so it can be filled in automatically for a "truly convenient" shopping experience.

Financial advisors often advise "out-of-control online shoppers" to
literally freeze their spending by putting their credit card in a plastic con-
tainer, filling it with water, and putting it in the freezer. The credit card
will be frozen in a block of ice, and not available for impromptu spending.
If you really want or need to purchase something, you will still want it
once the credit card has thawed, but you will have had time to think about
the purchase and make a quality decision. Impulse shopping can easily
wreck your budget and leave you with high credit card debt. In some cases,
it can even lead to financial ruin.

If you spend an inordinate amount of time shopping online, and
many people do, it is a good idea to stop for a while and think about your

priorities. Are you exchanging your life for shopping experiences? Your life is made up of moments. How many of those moments do you spend each week browsing online stores in search of items to purchase?

When shopping online, it is important to make sure you are buying from a reputable site. Check the return policy for the specific item you want to purchase. Read the reviews that other customers have posted for the item and for the company. Find out what the shipping cost is and how long it takes for your purchase to arrive at your house. Some companies advertise that they "usually process orders within twenty-four hours," but fail to tell you that while they may process the transaction within twenty-four hours, the item may not actually be shipped for three or four days, and then shipping time may be another seven to ten days. This information is particularly critical if you are ordering a gift that needs to arrive on time for someone's birthday or a holiday.

If you frequently shop online, check your online credit card statement throughout the month, particularly after buying things online, to make sure your credit card was correctly charged and not used for any unauthorized purchases.

Final Thoughts

Nazeefah and Nabeel,
*   When done smartly and safely, online shopping can save time and provide more choices. However, it should not be a constant activity that absorbs an inordinate amount of your time and money.*
Your Dad

22

IT HAS NOTHING TO DO WITH LUCK

Don't ever, ever believe anyone who tells you that you can
just get by, by doing the easiest thing possible. Because
there's always somebody behind you who really wants to
do what you're doing. And they're going to work harder
than you if you're not working hard.

— MARIA BARTIROMO

Confession #18

*Luck is overrated. When we make a plan and are willing to work hard to make the plan
happen, we usually see good results. I am proud to see that my children have developed
a strong work ethic. I do, however, remember when Nazeefah was participating in the
Jump Rope for Heart fundraiser at school. The goal was to win a bicycle by collecting the
most money for the charity. She assumed that the "bank of mom and dad" would bank-
roll the money and there would be no need to go door to door in the neighborhood to collect
charitable donations. Her luck ran out when she realized that Mom and Dad would not
help her reach her target. Instead, her own effort was required to earn her prize!*

Have you ever watched how people around you do their work? If
you take the time to pay attention to this, you will probably notice that

most people fall into one of two working camps—those who roll up their sleeves and get the job done and those who find every excuse possible not to work but want the results as if they had. Let's call the two camps "Camp Get it Done" and "Camp Wish it Were Done."

If we take a closer look, we can see some distinct differences between the work camps. In Camp Get it Done, we see people who show up on time and with a plan. They have the equipment or tools needed for the work and they are dressed appropriately for the work. The people in Camp Get It Done are mentally and physically prepared for what lies ahead. They are rested and ready to tackle the tasks they are trusted to complete. They understand their task and have a strategy for how they will do the work once they arrive at the work site. They encourage those with whom they are working and are helpful and cooperative with the team. The work goes smoothly and the people from Camp Get It Done complete their work on time without any major problems. They are free to move on with their day.

Not so with Camp Wish It Were Done. They aren't quite so "lucky." The people in this camp show up late, mumbling excuses about how they were up late watching a movie the previous night and their roommate forgot to wake them on time. (Haven't they heard of taking personal responsibility and setting their own alarm clock?)

Even though it is evident that certain tools and equipment are needed for the job, they arrive at the work site empty handed. They try to borrow equipment from team Camp Get It Done, but there isn't enough equipment to go around. Instead of considering that it is their responsibility to bring what they needed, they blame the people in Camp Get It Done for not bringing enough extra equipment to compensate for their lack of preparation. They waste a lot of time tracking down the tools they need to get the job done and start the job much later than scheduled.

The Camp Wish It Were Done people sleep too late to eat breakfast before work, so by midmorning, they are hungry. They abandon the job to go get food. Rather than eat and get back to work, they sit around talking after they eat, hoping someone will finish the work for them before they return to the work site. That doesn't happen.

Without a carefully thought-out plan, these people's work goes slowly and several time-consuming mistakes require do overs. Team morale dwindles as teammates blame one another for the mistakes. No one wants to take responsibility. Everyone moves slowly, trying to do as little as possible while expecting the others to do more than their fair share.

The group finally leaves the work site by midafternoon, all claiming that they have more important things to do. The job is left incomplete and the site is a mess. As they turn out the lights, they look over at the completed Camp Get It Done project, and say, "Those guys are really lucky."

The behavior and work ethics of the two teams illustrate the point. In school, the workplace, volunteer situations, and at home, you can recognize that careful planning and hard work bring about good results, while laziness, carelessness, and lack of planning yield the opposite. You reap what you sow: luck has nothing to do with it.

When things just seem to work out well for a particular person, other people may say, "Wow—that's one lucky person!" People have a tendency to look at the result of that person's careful planning and hard work, rather than all of the work that has led to the great results.

Here is another story to illustrate the point. Mike is six feet, three inches tall and muscular. He is good-looking and has a laid-back personality that makes people instantly like him when they meet him. He lives by the beach in a small coastal town.

Every day around two in the afternoon, Mike leashes his golden retriever and takes a run on the beach that is less than a block from his home. Sometimes his beautiful wife joins him. When people see Mike running on the beach every day, they automatically assume that he is a very lucky guy. They think he was born fit and handsome and lives an undemanding life by the beach. They think he's lucky enough to have a beautiful wife, a show-quality golden retriever, a house by the beach, a new car, and lots of free time. Since he runs in the early afternoon, they assume he doesn't work at a job and that his money came to him through wealthy parents. Every year, Mike and his wife take one quality vacation in another country. Their friends always say the same thing: "You're so lucky that you get to travel the world!"

It may appear that Mike lives a charmed, lucky life, but in reality, his life is the result of his actions and hard work. What people do not see is that when Mike was in high school, he determined what he wanted, created a plan, and worked hard to make that plan happen.

When his high school friends were hanging out for countless hours, playing video games, and talking nonsense, Mike was working for a local landscaper after school and during the summer. He had goals he wanted to reach that would require large sums of money. Rather than depending on his parents or someone else to give him the money, he knew the right thing was to work for it.

Even though he spent a lot of time working, Mike also volunteered at a local soup kitchen during the winter months when work was slower. At the soup kitchen, he met another volunteer that instantly captured his heart, and married his beautiful wife a few years later.

Rather than sit around during the winter months when he was off from work, Mike focused on his studies so that he could reach his goal to start a business. He learned how to write a business plan and find start-up funding, and figured out the most direct college path to prepare himself for his plan.

Mike liked technology and "stuff" every bit as much as his peers, but he knew that he had to prioritize if he wanted to reach his goals. Mike did not buy new electronics or the latest fashionable clothes every week when he got his paycheck. Instead, he went to some events, but he didn't go to every event just because the opportunity presented itself.

Mike didn't buy an expensive car and hand over a hefty chunk of his weekly pay to the bank for payments. He drove a modest, dependable truck that worked well for his landscaping job. He bought classic clothes that didn't quickly go out of style, and wore them until they were actually worn out. For entertainment, he checked out books he wanted to read from the public library and spent time with his close friends. He was creative with setting up fun, inexpensive dates with his girlfriend. Sure, he got teased a little for his thrifty ways and boring truck, but it was all in good fun, and he had bigger plans.

Mike deposited most of his paychecks into his savings account. It was all part of his plan to marry his sweetheart and start a business. He patiently worked hard through high school and college, adjusting his plan as needed to compensate for unexpected events and circumstances over which he had no control. There were some upsets and delays at various times that took him off schedule for a short while, but Mike kept his mind on his plan and continued to work toward it, no matter what else happened.

Mike developed good habits for taking care of himself. He realized that he was the only one who could make his life what he wanted it to be. He needed to be physically and mentally strong and alert. He exercised, ate healthy foods, and made sure he got plenty of sleep every night. He avoided the traps of alcohol, drugs, and late-night partying that seemed to ensnare so many of his peers. It was clear to him that he couldn't "soar with the eagles and hoot with the owls," as his dad liked to say. He had to make a choice to line up his actions with his long-term goals instead of choosing instant fun and gratification to the detriment of his long-term goals.

When Mike was twenty-four, he married the woman of his dreams, bought a modest beach house, and started a business that he could run from home. He set his alarm clock for 4:30 a.m. every morning and was at work by 5:30. He worked diligently until 1:30 p.m. every day, ate lunch, and hit the beach at 2:00 for a run.

Was Mike just a lucky person? No. He was an imperfect but hardworking person who decided on the kind of life he wanted and was willing to do what it took for this to become a reality. He did not depended on anyone else to make it happen for him, though he was smart enough to take good advice and support from those who offered it. He did not make excuses for why his life could not or would not happen. He did not feel "entitled" to a life that he wasn't willing to work for. He didn't give up when things were difficult, nor did he blame others for the things that did not work out as he wanted them to.

Final Thoughts

Dear Nazeefah and Nabeel,

No matter how much I wish that everything in your life would be perfect, I know that it won't happen. Life is messy, and somewhat unpredictable. We only have control over certain things. One of the things we do have control over is how well we plan and how hard we choose to work. How we choose to work can determine the outcome of our plans. Some of the best parental advice that I can give you is to always plan and always work hard for what you want to achieve. Always here to give advice.

Dad

PART THREE: FINANCIAL FUNDAMENTALS

The minute you get away from fundamentals—whether it's proper technique, work ethic or mental preparation—the bottom can fall out of your game, your schoolwork, your job, whatever you're doing.

— MICHAEL JORDAN

23

IMPORTANT STUFF IN A BOX

I am not interested in competing with anyone. I hope we
all make it.

— ERICA COOK

Confession #19

*Like most parents, we nagged our children to clean up after themselves and ensure that
their rooms were neat and organized. "What is the point of getting organized?" they
would say to me. At the time, the only point was for them to understand good hygiene
habits and tidiness. I soon realized that all those years of nagging them to keep their
rooms organized were for a purpose after all. The purpose was to develop good organizing
habits…habits that would influence the way they manage their money.*

As you grow older and become responsible for your own financial
matters, you will be required to keep track of important papers. This could
be a big change when you are accustomed to asking Mom or Dad to re-
trieve important documents that they have kept on file for you or just letting them handle the matters altogether.

An organization system will help you retain your sanity and protect
your documents. If you keep your important papers organized, you will

always have them available when they are needed and you won't have to worry about them getting lost or destroyed. This is critical. Inadequate record keeping makes you vulnerable to financial loss.

You don't have to be part financial whiz kid and part Martha Stewart to manage your financial records! All you need is an organized system that stores your papers/documents and accounts for your cash flow.

What kind of records are we talking about?

Personal documents can include any papers that you need to keep. For instance, items that you might need to use when applying for credit, renting a house, or applying for a job. These personal documents include your birth certificate, insurance card, copy of driver's license, insurance policies, deeds to property, investment records, last will and testament, medical records, high school and college transcripts, and family history records.

Financial documents could include savings and checking account records, including canceled checks. Keep all credit card transaction slips and monthly credit card statements. You will want to have a current credit report on file. You can obtain one free annual credit report by going to annualcreditreport.com and providing information to download a credit report. For security purposes, make sure you access this site by typing the URL into your browser rather than clicking on a link from another site.

Tax returns are important financial documents that you should keep on file for several years. You should also file your tax statements from your job as well as your paycheck stubs. You should also file your receipts, budget, accounting sheets, vehicle documents, warranties, mortgage documents, rental contracts, and passwords.

Where do you store the records?

Currently, it's becoming popular to store information in "the cloud." The positive side of storing records online is that you can access them on any of your devices (phone, tablet, or laptop) from any location as long as you have a Wi-Fi connection. This is very convenient if you are away from home and realize you need access to a financial document.

But there are some drawbacks as well when storing sensitive personal information online. The server may be considered secure, but there is always the possibility of the data being hacked and your financial records accessed and used. There is also a risk of the servers going down and being unable to access necessary documents at a critical time.

As an alternative, you can also simply scan and store documents on your computer hard drive and do your accounting on your computer with your own forms or with a program such as QuickBooks for personal use. This is less convenient than the cloud because you can only access the records when you have your computer with you, but the records are fairly secure if you use encryption.

Most people nowadays use online banking. Often, these individuals maintain their credit card accounts online. The accounts are excellent for quick access to account records, statements, and such. It's rather nice to have someone else do the bookkeeping for you! But there is also a little less peace of mind when you know there is a risk of your information disappearing. What would happen if all of your online account records suddenly disappeared? It's un likely, but it's possible. Would you know how much money you have in savings? Would you have any proof that you have any money in a savings account? Would you have any proof that you paid your last credit card payment or electric bill if you could not access accounts online?

Mentioning this is not for the sake of stirring fear or creating any panic. It is something for you to take into consideration. Many people, particularly older individuals who feel uncomfortable having all their records be kept digitally, may choose to keep additional paper records, in addition to online services. They maintain a paper check register, so they always know their deposits, withdrawals, and current balance. (If you have never used a paper check register, ask your bank for one.) They may pay their utility bills online for convenience, but they print a paper receipt of the payment and keep it on file. The paper records are good backups in case anything goes wrong with the online accounts.

On the other hand, a file box with paper files is subject to theft, fire, and natural disasters, so the online records can also act as a backup for paper records. Therefore, having your records stored "in the cloud" and on your computer hard drive as well as in a physical file box gives you the best aspects of all options.

The most important documents, particularly the ones that cannot be replaced, should be kept in a safety deposit box at a bank, with copies stored at home and on your computer.

Final Thoughts

Dear Nazeefah and Nabeel,

I want you to grow in wisdom and responsibility. Part of becoming responsible for your finances is learning to maintain accurate financial records and keep your documents in order. To do that, you must exercise a certain level of organization. The method you use for storing your financial documents is less important than the fact that you have a method and use it. Adopting the habit of keeping all of your important papers together will eliminate a huge contributor of stress from your life.

Yours,

Dad

24

"BUDGET" ISN'T A BAD WORD

A budget is telling your money where to go, instead of
wondering where it went.

— DAVE RAMSEY

Confession #20

*When we were on vacation, my kids would order room service without understanding
that mom and dad had planned the vacation on a budget. They saw the vacation as a
"reward." I'm not sure for what it was for, but they felt entitled to spend as much they
could in the shortest possible time.*

By the time people reach their late teens and young adulthood, they
probably have realized that self-imposed restrictions help them manage
their life in a responsible manner. A budget is a self-imposed spending
management system, designed to help you use your money responsibly.
People who use budgets have far less financial worry in their lives than
those who do not.

Budgeting is not an outdated concept. It is every bit as relevant today
as it was in previous generations. Creating a budget indicates that you realize you need to apply structure and discipline to your finances. It may

mean that you are smart enough to realize that you need a clear picture of how much money you have coming in and where your money goes once it leaves your bank account.

What follows are lame excuses for not using a budget.

I don't have the same income every month.

Not everyone has the type of job that provides the same income from one month to the next. Jobs with hourly pay and varying hours each week, such as retail jobs, can make budgeting trickier, but not impossible. Creating a budget based on averages is better than not having a budget. You can adjust a budget as needed when your income varies.

I have plenty of money, so there is no need to budget.

It is a myth that only poor people need to budget their money. Everyone needs a budget, regardless of whether they have a meager allowance, a fat bank account, or an average wage. Your financial status does not alter the purpose that a budget serves.

I don't have enough money to budget.

No matter how small your income, budgeting is crucial. Whether your income is $500 per month or $5,000 per month, you still need to know how much money is coming in and how to distribute it for maximum benefit.

Creating a budget takes too much time.

Just skipping one evening of TV, shopping at the mall, or hanging out with friends will provide you enough time to create a budget. And in the end, the budget can save time, as you will have a visual record of your finances to refer to as needed.

Creating a budget is too complicated.

Anyone can create a simple, no-nonsense budget with just a few steps. In fact, let us get started with that now!

❖ Gather your monthly bills, review the debit card and check purchases on your bank statement, and go through your receipts for the previous month. You will gain an accurate idea of how much you are spending on a month-to-month basis.

❖ Start a new paper or electronic document and set up income and expenses categories in two columns. Your income column should include your take-home pay after taxes, health insurance premiums, and any other deductions. It should also include any other monthly income that you receive. Examples are allowance, support from a parent, income from a second job, investments, tips from service jobs, or passive streams of income.

❖ In the expenses column, list all of your monthly expenditures. Fixed expenses are the expenses that you have every month; they are usually the same or very close to the same amount every month. These may include housing, utilities, debts, insurance premiums, transportation costs, groceries, cell phone, membership fees, and savings.

❖ Variable expenses are the ones that are not set expenses every month. These expenses may include entertainment, clothing and shoes, grooming, school supplies, and gifts.

❖ Once you are certain that you have listed all of your income and expenses, add up the income and expense categories and subtract the total expenses from the total income to arrive at your net income. Your net income should be a positive number. If it's negative, you don't have enough income to cover your monthly expenses. Budgets don't lie!

If your net income is negative, go over all of your expenses and figure out how you can lower them. This may mean decreasing your spending on unnecessary purchases. Adjust the budget accordingly.

If your net income is positive, good job! But rather than spend the money, leave a little to cushion your checking account and transfer the rest to savings!

Creating a budget is a good thing, but it does nothing for you if you put it away and don't discipline yourself to live by it. So always keep it handy. Make a few copies to keep in your wallet, your car, and at your desk. Check it often, making sure to stay on track.

Track your spending by writing down each purchase you make and the amount. Save receipts. If you budgeted $25 per week for lattes, stop buying lattes when you reach that amount! If your clothing budget is $150 per month and you like a jacket that is $200, you must choose either to pass up the new item, or to trade two weeks of lattes to afford it.

Budgeting is a foundational principle of money management. Do not miss this crucial step for lack of discipline.

Final Thoughts

Dear Nazeefah and Nabeel,

Setting boundaries for yourself is a necessary part of living a responsible life. Boundaries can be seen as something that prevents you from doing what you want, or as something that protects you. A budget is merely a tool that allows you to take control of your finances and protects you from spending too much.

Use a budget wisely and it will help you reach you goals.

Love,

Dad

25

DEBT IS SUCH A BORING WORD

If everyone demanded peace instead of another television
set, then there'd be peace.

— JOHN LENNON

Confession #21

I took it for granted that my kids understood the meaning and consequences of debt. I could not have been more wrong. There was no need for them to understand the consequences of debt because Mom and Dad would take care of any monies owed. Debt is probably the most dismal subject to speak to your kids about, and our family was no different. After all, you figure that they will have enough time to understand debt when they are older.

Debt is one of those words that most people would rather ignore, but when discussing finances, it can't be ignored. Unmanaged debt can have a long-lasting negative effect on your finances, lifestyle, retirement, and peace of mind. Bad debt management has ruined people, businesses, and even cities and countries.

As previously stated, all debt is not bad debt, and acquiring debt can be necessary and even useful at times. The important things to remember are that you should only accumulate good debt—the kind that brings and increases value—and avoid bad debt—the kind that costs you money with no return on your investment. Also, keep in mind that even debt that adds value has to be debt that you can afford.

Debt that you cannot afford to repay is not debt that you should be willing to acquire. Careful planning can help you avoid debt that you cannot afford. Whether you are shopping for a mortgage or a college loan, utilize loan calculator tools to help. These will allow you to see precisely what your total debt amount and monthly payments will be after all loan-related costs, such as interest and insurance, are factored in. Once you determine whether you can afford the debt, realize that even if you can afford to pay the monthly payments, you may not be able to afford the impact it will have on your credit rating if your debt-to-income ratio is affected.

Look at the bottom line and see if it is affordable for you. Be realistic. It is easy to be overly optimistic about something that you hope will work in your favor. It can be easy to look at only the positive aspects of your current financial situation and ignore the negative possibilities that may exist. It may also help to have another objective opinion. Don't hesitate to talk with a financial advisor, a wise friend who is financially savvy, or your parents.

Never let debt dominate your life. If you acquire more debt than you can manage, make every effort to eliminate or pay down the debt as quickly as possible. Don't try to ignore it or be unrealistically optimistic about it. Take action. Otherwise, you will begin to serve the debt instead of it serving you.

Here are some tips for eliminating or reducing debt.

Don't incur new debt unless absolutely necessary.

Use discipline. Even if it means getting by with an older car, eschewing a new seasonal wardrobe, cutting back on holiday spending, or foregoing a vacation, pay off existing debt and choose to be debt-free rather than incurring more.

Continue to fund your emergency savings account.

You don't want to have to incur debt to handle emergencies.

Be careful with credit cards.

Credit card debt can rack up hundreds of dollars per year in interest, especially if you have more than one or two credit cards. Sometimes, it is best to focus on paying off one credit card at a time rather than attempting multiple payoffs. Ask your credit card provider to lower your interest rate. The company may not do it, but it does not hurt to ask. If you cannot pay your credit card balance in full each month, pay two monthly minimum payments instead of one to reduce your daily monthly balance and interest.

Pay off all high-interest debt.

Any accounts you have with an interest rate over 10 percent must be eliminated as quickly as possible. Focus first on doing away with the one with the highest interest rate.

Cut expenses if you can.

Distinguish the needs from the wants in terms of expenses and cut the wants.

Final Thoughts

Dear Nazeefah and Nabeel,

May you do what successful people do—create only good debt, and manage or eliminate your debt when possible. By doing this, your life will be less stressful and more enjoyable. What parent doesn't want that for his or her children? While eliminating bad debt and living

*freely with manageable or zero debt may seem impossible when you
first try it, people do it every day — and you can, too!
With hope and belief for your ongoing financial health,
Dad*

26

KNOW GOOD DEBT AND BAD DEBT

Debt is the slavery of the free.

— PUBLILIUS SYRUS

Confession #22

I had thought that since my children had no need to understand debt, learning the difference between good debt and bad debt was moot.

Few people who live "normal" lives escape debt completely. At the very least, most people incur debt for mortgages, student loans, and life events. Such life events may include getting married, having a child, and starting a new business. It is easy to understand that these debts are entered into for the acquisition of good things. All of the things associated with them have value that extends beyond excessive materialism. They all contribute to the quality of life and offer a return on the investment.

When students take out college loans, they are investing in their future career. There are many jokes about starving students, but we can learn something from university students who are willing to invest so heavily in their future. We learn that it is OK to acquire debt to reach long-term goals.

Ideally, from a financial perspective, when a person invests in real estate, the property should increase in value as the years pass. The property should remain an asset. Another positive outcome for the purchase of property can be the stability of a home and memories created. When children grow up in the family home and fill the place with precious memories, parents cherish the memories throughout their golden years. They can look back and know they made a good choice in securing a comfortable home for raising their family.

On the other hand, there is such a thing as bad debt. Bad debt tends to cost one more than it should in the end. Bad debt is when transactions and loans are carried out for temporary items, or things that have little to no future return or value.

To a certain extent, everyone must decide for him or herself what is good debt or bad debt, although there are some classically bad debts. To the exhausted person who has worked hard for a few years without a vacation, taking a loan to go on a cruise may be a good investment that pays off with renewed health and enthusiasm for life. For someone who vacations frequently, however, going into debt for yet another vacation would probably be frivolous.

One thing you should avoid when determining whether a debt is good or bad is justifying bad purchases or lying to yourself about purchases. People have a tendency to justify bad purchases by telling themselves that they deserve to have what they want. You deserve good things, but you also deserve to not have unmanageable debt in your future. You deserve the freedom to choose your path without being hindered or tied down by bad debt. Too often, people take on bad debt when they are young, and this affects their ability to make choices for many years afterward. Their actions are limited by their burden of debt.

Discontentment and lack of gratitude are often the genesis of bad debt. Discontentment can be a tricky thing; it is not good to be content with mediocrity and never strive to do your best to become a better person, but it is good to be content with what you have as you work toward your goals. Practicing gratitude keeps you content and goes a long way toward protecting you from bad debt.

Final Thoughts

Dear Nazeefah and Nabeel,

May you incur only good debt in your lives, and have the wisdom to know good debt from bad debt!

Before taking on any debt, stop and consider whether it is good debt or bad debt. If you are not sure, speak to someone who can help you see the situation more objectively.

I'm always here to help.

Dad

27

WHAT IS A CREDIT REPORT, AND WHY SHOULD YOU CARE?

Creditors have better memories than debtors.

—Benjamin Franklin

Confession #23

I didn't know what a credit report was until I first applied for a mortgage. Nobody had prepared me for an "adult report card." I thought that my days of receiving report cards on my performance were over. How could I expect my kids to understand the ins and outs of a credit report?

As parents, our role is to protect our children from danger. From a young age, we have protected them from getting hit by cars, teaching them to look both ways before crossing the street. But as you move into adulthood, a new kind of danger lurks: the danger of not understanding a credit report. A what, you ask? A credit report is like your high school report card. Just as poor grades can negatively affect your academic options, a poor credit history can have far-reaching negative consequences for your money and investments. Your credit report can open and close doors for you. Responsible financial behavior will help you keep those doors open and present opportunities.

A credit report is a report available to outside parties with your consent containing information about your credit, bill repayment history, and the status of your credit accounts. This information includes how often you make your payments on time, how much credit you have available, how much credit you are using, and whether an agency is collecting on money you owe.

Your credit score is like a report card for how well you've managed your credit. Instead of a letter grade, you are assigned a credit score number based on specific factors.

The reason we helped my daughter Nazeefah to apply for a credit was to help her establish a credit history. We knew that by managing her credit card responsibly, the banks would look at her credit applications favorably. She would need a good credit score later in life when she made large purchases, like a home and car.

If you do not manage your finances wisely, it will reflect poorly on your credit report. The consequences are that you may be denied additional credit or turned down for a home loan. If you have a poor credit history but manage to get a loan, your interest rate will be higher than if you had a good credit history. When that ends up costing you hundreds of thousands of dollars, the interest rate *really* matters. On a mortgage of $350,000, the lifetime difference that you would pay between 3 percent loan and 5 percent loan is around $150,000. We're not talking pocket change when it comes to interest rates on mortgages!

What is a good credit score?

As far as credit scores, here are some guidelines that banks use to loan money:

- ❖ *300–580*: You'll be denied credit, or will only be approved for the very highest, most costly interest rates.
- ❖ *581–650*: You may qualify for credit at high interest rates.
- ❖ *651–710*: You'll qualify for credit at moderate interest rates.

❖ *711–750*: You'll qualify for credit at competitive interest rates.

❖ *751 and up*: You'll get the most competitive, lowest interest rates on the market.

Avoid the following three mistakes.

1- Paying only part of the balance owing on your card

Controlling when you use a credit card and when you pay cash is key to good financial management. When you charge a purchase to your credit card, you enjoy a 21 day "interest holiday," on one condition: you must pay the FULL balance owing on your purchase before the due date shown on your statement.

Example: You buy a laptop computer, costing $700, in September. When you receive your credit card statement in early October, you must pay the $700 in full before the due date shown on your statement. This is the only way to avoid paying interest. If you pay only $500, you will be charged interest on the full amount of your purchase, i.e. $700, not just on the $200 balance. This could cost you around $12 if the interest rate on your card is 18%.

Advice: Put some money aside before making a large purchase. That way, you will avoid paying interest charges.

2- Paying your bills late

Is it all that serious if you delay a day or two beyond the due date shown on your credit card statement? The answer is: Yes! Not only will you pay interest on the total balance of your purchases, but your credit record will show the late payment. Late payment signifies that you have failed to fulfill your part of the contract with the credit card issuer. This could adversely affect your credit score and your "borrowing" image.

Advice: If you are unable to pay the full balance on your account on the due date, make at least the minimum payment before that date. As soon as you have more funds, pay the remaining balance in full.

3- *Asking for a cash advance*

A cash advance means withdrawing cash from your credit card account at an automatic teller machine. This is a loan, and there is no holiday on the interest. As a result, you will start incurring charges on the date of your withdrawal.

Advice: Before taking a cash advance, review your other options, such as borrowing funds from your parents. If you have already taken a cash advance on your credit card, repay the amount you borrowed as quickly as possible, in order to pay less interest.

Final Thoughts

Dean Nazeefah and Nabeel,

The difference between a school report card and a credit report card is that a bad credit report can remain on your financial record for many years and may cost you money in the long run.

Protect your credit worthiness by being responsible and taking your finances seriously.

I learned about credit reports very late in life. I'm here to help you navigate the murky waters of credit reports sooner than I did.

Love,
Dad

28

CREDIT CARDS AND INDEPENDENCE

Procrastination is like a credit card: it's a lot of fun until
you get the bill.

—CHRISTOPHER PARKER

Confession #24

*I remember the day fondly. I was twenty-one years old when I applied and received my
first credit card. I was so excited because this shiny card gave me confidence and elevated
my status among friends and family. That was until I received my first bill. Somehow,
the card no longer looked so shiny.*

*As my kids enter the "adult world," I want them to have a firm under-
standing of how credit cards work. Since credit cards can be such a big part of
managing finances, you must understand the fundamentals of having and using
them.*

When my daughter entered university, we thought it would be a good
idea for her to manage her first credit card. So, just like the "sex education" lecture, I sat down and spoke to her about managing her credit card.
Some of the points I went over with her follow.

❖ Credit cards are like sharp knives. They are wonderful tools, but they can damage you badly if you use them incorrectly.

❖ Credit is not "free" money. It must always be paid back.

❖ Paying only the minimum each month can drag payments out for many years.

❖ The credit card company charges a fee if the payment is late and doing so can increase the interest rate.

❖ Credit card companies make money by charging you a fee to participate and a very high interest rate if you do not settle the full amount owed.

❖ Credit cards can be incredibly useful tools for convenience when doing many routine tasks, like buying gas.

❖ Using your credit card can help maintain good credit history so that you can get good rates on a mortgage or line of credit. But always follow the golden rule: Pay off the whole balance each month.

❖ The trick with credit cards is to not allow them to trick you into a false sense of financial confidence. When you buy something with a credit card, it is not immediately reflected in the balance of your checking account. That fact can often lull people into a false sense of financial security, which can lead to overspending.

By continuing to reinforce these messages, my hope is that eventually you will fully practice them.

Final Thoughts

Dear Nazeefah and Nabeel,

Once you both get a full set of credit cards, my hope is that you will value your independence and enjoy managing your finances. Once you do, do not allow a shiny credit card to divert you from your financial plan. *Set boundaries that you will not cross. A desire to maintain your financial independence will motivate you to do whatever it takes.*

Love always,
Dad

29

HOW UNMANAGEABLE DEBT IS CREATED

Debt-free…the new status symbol of choice.

— Dave Ramsey

Confession #25

I have had several conversations with my kids about managing their credit cards, as well as the difference between wants and needs. In the process, I have been pleasantly surprised how well they have managed their credit cards and how paranoid they both are about paying the bills off in full every month. However, there was one time when I had to bail them out. Confusing one's wants with one's needs can easily lead to unnecessary debt, and unnecessary debt can lead to poor quality of life. My wife and I want our children to live a quality life, unhindered by debt.

Many people make the mistake of thinking that they need to have more or do more than their monthly income will allow them to afford. Because they have not learned the difference between a want and a need, or do not practice patience, delayed gratification, and discipline, such individuals buy and do the things they want "on credit." Instead of saving or simply admitting that they cannot afford something, they borrow money to get it right then. Usually, this means using a credit card to make a purchase, but it can also include borrowing money from a bank (or friends and family) and promising to pay it back in monthly increments. It can also mean purchasing "pay later" services, where no money is due at the time of sign-up, but the bill comes next month.

If you are thinking that sounds like a great way to always get what you want, think again. There are serious issues with this plan! Part of growing up and becoming an independent adult is managing money without depending on credit or the financial assistance of others. Accepting that you cannot always have what you want is a big step toward financial responsibility.

Another thing to consider is what will happen when you keep borrowing and creating more bills until your bills exceed your ability to make the monthly payments. The result is unmanageable debt.

When people live from paycheck to paycheck due to poor spending habits, they often reach a point when their income has to increase or they will be unable to pay their monthly bills. When one is a child under their parents' roof, with all of their needs supplied by their parents, the consequences of spending all of their monthly allowance on something frivolous may not truly matter. However, as an adult, acquiring too much debt can have severe consequences. For instance, when adults continue to accrue more debt than they can repay, they can lose their house, get evicted from their apartment, mar their credit score, or be sued in a court of law for payments owed.

When you have more monthly expenses than monthly income, you cannot pay all of your bills—or at least not all on time. You may be able to juggle the bills for a month or two, but sooner or later (and usually sooner than you think), one will fall. And when it does, you'll shake your head and wonder why you created the imbalance in your life by allowing your expenses to become greater than your income.

Final Thoughts

Dear Nazeefah and Nabeel,

One simple warning: Your bills will pile up quickly. Don't allow the burden of unmanageable debt to crush your economic life. Do whatever it takes to cut spending and, if it comes to it, get your debt down to a manageable level.

You have a long financial road ahead of you. By following a few simple precautions, you can keep financial woes and debts at bay.
Your partner in financial planning,
Dad

30

THAT FEELING OF BEING DEBT-FREE: PRICELESS

New Louis Vuitton purse: $2,480
New iPad Air: $699
New Armani suit: $999
Not buying any of the above and remaining debt-free: PRICELESS

Confession #26

Debt can be a foreign concept to kids. After all, what debt does a fifteen-year-old have? When Mother's Day comes along, I have always encouraged my children to get mom a gift from the heart, because gifts from the heart never go out of style. But, in this overly-commercialized world, helping my children get their mom a gift seemed to be what was expected. The big mistake I made was buying the Mother's Day gift for my kids to give to their mom, instead of them figuring out the gift for themselves and, paying it with their own money. I had fallen victim to the oldest trick in the book!

Many people aspire to be free from debt. This is not always easy to do. When a person starts from a position of debt, it requires tremendous willpower and determination to extricate oneself from the situation and achieve his or her goal. But that said, there is no greater feeling (apart from witnessing the birth of your children, of course) than lifting yourself by your bootstraps and getting out of debt. That feeling is priceless.

If you are in this situation, here are a few perks of getting out of debt that should help you become motivated to achieve debt freedom and become truly happy.

You won't have to worry about money.

When you aren't indebted to anyone, you will be left with more money for yourself. True, you can't buy happiness with money, but being miserably broke all the time doesn't do you any favors either! Having fewer worries about money will make you happier.

There will be no need to panic when sudden expenses come up.

If you suddenly become sick and require treatment, you will have to spend money for the medications and doctor visits. If this happens while you are in debt, you feel the stress of both poor health and poor finances.

You will have something to look forward to when you retire.

If you are approaching retirement but are still in debt, then it could seem as if there's nothing to look forward to. If you clear all your debts before retirement, then your golden years will be a haven of comfort and relaxation – as they should be.

You will have fewer things to worry about.

Monitoring and paying bills takes up a lot of time. You also have to think a lot about deadlines and schedules. The more debt you have, the more things you have to keep track of. Life will definitely be easier if you become debt-free.

You will impart a valuable life lesson to your children.

Once you have a family and are raising children, their childhood years will be more carefree when their parents aren't stressed about being in debt. You will be showing your children the perfect example of how to manage their finances so they don't end up in debt themselves when they reach adulthood.

You will be able to help other people.

When you have more money for yourself and less for debtors, you can share the wealth with those in need. You can donate to charitable organizations if you don't have to pay up to loan sharks and credit card companies every month.

You will feel empowered.

If you can achieve your goal of being debt-free, then you will believe that you can do anything.

You won't be stressed out.

Being debt-free lets you live life freely and without worry. Bob Marley sings, "Don't worry, be happy." If you are in debt, you may find this hard to do.

You will be able to build your own wealth.

Instead of giving your money to debtors, you will be able to begin investing and saving more in the process. Better yet, invest wisely and you may even be able to see your money grow exponentially. If you can provide for yourself and your family, then your life will be more comfortable.

Final Thoughts

Dear Nazeefah and Nabeel,

I cannot guarantee that you will be eternally happy without debts, but if you have no debt to worry about, your chance of experiencing real happiness is much higher. Do not underestimate the value of being happy and free from worry. I recall the bright smile on your faces when you both paid for my first Father's Day gift from your savings. You did not ask mommy or I for a loan. It gave you both so much pleasure to purchase something with your own money. As you get older, you will understand the value of not stretching out your hand to anybody and being able to remain debt-free. There is no greater pleasure than standing on your own two feet and doing things for yourself.

Looking forward to a long road of your financial independence and growth to come.

Dad

31

DEBT IS THE SAME FOR THE WEALTHY AND THE NOT-SO-WEALTHY

A debt may get mouldy, but it never decays.

— CHINUA ACHEBE

Confession #27

I'm afraid I perpetuated the myth for my kids that all financially successful people have big houses and fancy cars. This was before I studied the financial habits of Warren Buffet. He is one of the richest people in the world, but he lived in the same house for most of his adult life. He bought his house in 1958 for $31,500. What does Warren Buffet's house tell you about wealthy he is? Nothing. His house does not define who he is or what is important to him.

The only similarity between the rich and the poor is debt equality. Equality between different income levels seems like a myth, but the similarities are haunting when it comes to debt. When a family struggles financially with their debt load, it does not matter how much they earn.

I can hear you thinking, "How can that be true?"

You can get into debt, a company can get into debt, and so can a family. It makes no difference who or what you are. Debt is not picky, and it will find you.

Let me illustrate an idea.

The Lee household has an income of $200,000, and the Smith household has an income of $50,000. Both families are struggling with debt and both have debt levels double their annual household income. Both have debt but in different amounts.

This may surprise you, but the steps necessary to repair their debt are the same for both families — even though the amounts are vastly different. It doesn't matter how much or how little you make; financial success is achieved by spending less than you earn...no ifs, ands, or buts about it. If you make $50,000 a year, you will never improve your situation until you learn to live on less than $50,000 a year. If you make $200,000 a year, you will never improve your situation until you learn to live on less than $200,000 a year.

The solution is the same; only the dollar amounts are different. Both families are equally overwhelmed, paralyzed, and unable to move forward. The feeling of desperation is the same.

No matter how much money you make, having high levels of debt can be devastating to your future. The interest payments alone will eat away at your disposable income; taking away all of life's little pleasures.

Paying off high-interest debt as quickly as possible without incurring further debt must be your number-one priority. While faster is not always better, in this situation faster is — without a doubt — the best choice.

Always set aside money toward an emergency fund. If you don't have an emergency fund, you will be forced to go into unnecessary debt when you do have an emergency, and trust me, an emergency will definitely be heading your way eventually.

It doesn't matter how much or how little you make; you will eventually spend more money than you should based on your wants, rather than needs. We all do — myself included. We buy things on credit because we want them right away, not appreciating how this has become a completely normal behavior in our lives and that living without these wants seems difficult. Managing your wants and needs requires patience and planning.

The good news is that you can always change things. There is no financial hole too deep to dig yourself out of, no life that can't be altered to make it possible to recover financially. You can do this.

Final Thoughts

Dear Nazeefah and Nabeel,

Debt is the great equalizer. It is not how much you earn but how much you have at the end of the month that matters. If you always spend less than you earn, you will eliminate debt.

With a little self-awareness and precaution, you can stay ahead of the game.
Dad

32

NO WORRIES...RETIREMENT IS A LONG WAY AWAY

Based on my calculations, I can retire five years after
I die.

— Unknown

Confession #28

When I was still a twenty-something student, retirement was the last thing on my mind. I had grown up in a household of entrepreneurs, where retirement was never discussed. I started way too late saving for my retirement and would have been far better off if I had been given sound advice at a young age

Plan for retirement early and consistently. You are responsible for your retirement and should not depend on the government to take care of you in your old age.

When you are young, carefree, and unconcerned about your basic needs, retirement is probably the last thing on your mind.

According to statistics, only 28 percent of young adults under age twenty-five contribute to their retirement. Make yourself the exception to this statistic! That would place you far ahead of everyone else when it comes to saving for retirement, which means more money for yourself down the road.

Now that I have your attention, let me show you some of the benefits that come from early retirement planning. There are tons of information out there about how much to save for retirement, when to begin saving, and the tax implications of retirement.

Forget all of that. Here are some simple rules to live by when it comes to retirement planning.

Start early! Spread the challenges and savings over your whole life.

Spreading out your retirement contributions will allow you to make the process less stressful. It is possible, after all, to start saving at a young age without giving up life's little pleasures! Also, don't, spend more than you earn now, making the assumption that you will be able to put aside all the money at age sixty-five. Take care of your retirement planning equally throughout your life.

Saving and planning for retirement are two different things.

Begin saving at a young age, but start making retirement plans as you enter different stages of life.

Save early. Save often.

Even a very small amount saved for retirement can grow significantly by the time you retire. Every little bit helps.

Start with 5 percent.

Invest at least 5 percent of your monthly income toward retirement when you first begin investing. Increase it to 7 percent and then 10 percent as your income increases. Never dip into your retirement fund before you retire.

Maximize your retirement contributions and always take advantage of your company matching option, if offered.

If all you do is follow these simple rules, you will already be far ahead of your peers. You'll even be able to take care of your parents in their old age!

Final Thoughts

Dear Nazeefah and Nabeel,

There is no mandatory retirement age any longer. Decide on a retirement age and work toward that goal. Retirement may seem like a long way away for young people, but it's never too early to get started! In the twenty-first century, people can retire at sixty-five, or work as long as they like. You can also choose to retire at forty-five because you have decided how you want to spend the best years of your life. Whichever you choose, though, you need to start with a retirement plan.

I'm sure this is only the start of many talks on retirement that we will have in the years to come. My hope is to start your thinking in this direction as early as possible.

May we look toward your future together.
Dad

33

EMERGENCY? WHAT EMERGENCY (FUND)?

The time to repair the roof is when the sun is shining.

— JOHN F. KENNEDY

Confession #29

In December 2013, our family experienced the worst ice storm in living memory. Ice and snow caused power outages in our area, and we were without heat, power, or communication for five days. We were definitely not prepared. My kids' worst fears had been realized. No cell phone coverage, no Internet. They had to use words and communicate with people, who were no longer on the other side of an electronic device!

You cannot stop an ice storm from destroying trees and power lines, but you can be ready with an emergency kit and supplies to deal with the aftermath when it does. In the same way, you may not be able to prevent – or predict – a financial storm that hits your life, but you can have a plan to deal with it if, and when, it does. As a young adult, your plan should be more sophisticated than calling Mom and Dad!

You are truly fortunate to have access to the miracles of modern medicine and technology. Our society is safer and healthier, and people are living longer than ever before. There are national early-warning systems for weather-related emergencies, smoke alarms in our homes to warn us of potential fires, and security alarms to warn us if an intruder attempts to gain access to our homes. Even our cars have convenient computers that warn us when oil and gas levels are low. Yes, we are fully warned!

And yet emergencies still strike. And when they do, they demand our immediate attention and action. Again, we cannot know when financial emergencies will strike, but we can make sure we're prepared when they do.

Create a savings plan.

You may not want to be told to save money while you're young; you have a long life ahead of you to save, so why should you worry about it now? Keep in mind that you are not just saving for old age. You need to save for emergencies, too. Emergencies come in all shapes and sizes. Some emergencies – say, a broken toilet or dishwasher – only set you back a couple of hundred dollars. Others, however, may require that you quickly come up with thousands of dollars.

If you face a major economic emergency without adequate preparation, your life can change dramatically for the worse. A good family friend who is financially disciplined and conservative had to delay his dreams of early retirement because he was not prepared for financial emergencies. In the space of three months, he had to replace his roof, the engine of his paid-off car ceased to function the week after the warranty expired, and his son underwent an emergency appendectomy. When it rains, it most definitely pours.

Saving is the first step to achieving economic security, and it is your most important strategy to weather an economic storm. It is crucial to have emergency savings that would cover all personal and household expenses, as well as bills and obligations, for at least three to six months.

Saving is easy to talk about, but harder to actually do. The action of setting aside money does not happen by accident. It requires commitment and sacrifices. If you develop the habit of saving for an emergency as well as for your long-term goals, it will become second nature to you to save a part of your income regularly.

If your current income doesn't permit you to create an emergency fund, you may need to find a creative way to increase your income. This could include taking a part-time job in addition to your regular job or starting a small service-side business such as tutoring or dog walking. Think about how you can use your talents, such as writing, computer support for seniors, or teaching or graphic design, to earn extra money. You can also earn extra cash to put into savings if you have high-ticket toys, electronics, cars, and other things in your home that you no longer want or need. Consider selling the items and putting all the cash in savings.

Cut expenses.

This is one of the best ways to accumulate more income for savings. Take a serious look at where you spend money each week. How much do you "waste" that could go into your savings fund? If you start saving those five-dollar bills that are so easily and quickly spent on trivial items, it will add up quickly over a month's time. For example, I save my spare change daily and on my birthday each year I break open the jar of coins to see how much I have collected. This past year I collected over $400.

Like most people, our family has excessive services that we pay for but do not use, or can do without. Do we really need nine hundred cable TV channels, or one thousand cell phone minutes, or a daily newspaper that we never read?

If you have debt, try to pay it off as quickly as possible and put the monthly payment in your emergency savings account. The amount of interest you pay can increase your emergency fund significantly.

Keep your accounts separate, but accessible.

Your emergency funds should be easily accessible, but also kept separate from your other accounts. If your emergency fund is lumped in with monthly expense funds in your regular checking account, you may be tempted to spend it on something besides emergencies. You may get a false sense of having more spending money available than you actually have. But if you keep the funds in your long-term savings accounts, you may not be able to access it quickly for an emergency. It is best to have a separate account specifically for emergency funds. I prefer to keep my emergency funds at a separate bank entirely.

In addition to an emergency fund account, it is a good idea to have access to cash at home. It may seem a bit old fashioned, but you really never know what might happen.

Although you can never be prepared for everything, you can do your best to prepare with an emergency fund.

Final Thoughts

Dear Nazeefah and Nabeel,

You never know when an emergency will strike. Begin preparing early. Once the emergency happens, it is too late! Be smart, be creative, and be faithful with your emergency savings plan. A little rain must fall in everyone's life, and so it shall be with you.

Sometimes we can look to the sky and see the rain coming. But other times, the sky opens up without warning and torrential rains catch us off-guard. We definitely live in uncertain times. I hope to teach you to keep your eyes open but to also prepare for what you may not be able to see coming. As you develop your own finances, it is important to keep them in good order.

Remember, always hope for the best, but prepare for the worst. The most important thing to remember about emergencies is that once they hit, it is too late to prepare. Preparation implies taking action before the emergency happens.

Your mother and I have done our best to prepare you to avoid hardship, but now it is time to help you to prepare for the emergencies that will inevitably arise.

Sincerely,

Dad

34

EVERYBODY NEEDS A PLACE TO LIVE

The land is the only thing in the world worth working
for, worth fighting for, worth dying for, because it's the
only thing that lasts.

— MARGARET MITCHELL, *GONE WITH THE WIND*

Confession #30

*I began to invest in real estate very late in life. The main reason was that I did not have
a mentor to teach and guide me. "I did not know what I did not know," as they say. I
also did not have the knowledge and skills to fully understand how patience in the real
estate market could benefit me long term and help me to be financially free.*

The secret to acquiring wealth is through real estate. The economy
may rise and fall, but real estate will remain one of the most reliable investments. The reason is simple: *everybody needs a place to live.* When you
invest in real estate, your goal is to put your money to work today and to
make it grow so that you have more money in the future. Investing in real
estate can be an overwhelming thought for many people. The idea of finding a good property in a good neighborhood with a growing population,

and THEN finding a trustworthy renter can seem daunting. But as overwhelming as it may seem, with a little effort comes great reward.

As communities grow, so too does the value of property. And the greater the demand, the higher the value of the property. History has shown that real estate prices have continued to increase steadily over the years. The longer you hold onto your investment property, the higher your returns could be.

Purchasing and then renting an apartment is a good start toward property ownership. The rent paid by your tenants will be applied toward your mortgage on the property. There is nothing better than somebody else paying off your home.

Some of the benefits of owning real estate follow:

❖ *Taxes*: A number of deductions can be claimed on your tax return, such as for the cost of the interest paid on the loan, repairs and maintenance, property taxes, insurance, agent's fees, travel to and from the property to facilitate repairs, and depreciation. Also, when you own an income property, the interest on the mortgage payments is tax deductible. All this will help you save money when it comes to tax time.

❖ *Leverage*: The ability to invest a small amount towards owning something large is powerful. This means that a small amount of capital in your account can control a larger amount in the market. Real estate delivers the greatest opportunity to use the power of leverage. You can purchase a $200,000 property with only a small deposit. No other investment allows you to do that.

❖ *Control over your investment*: If you own and manage your own property, you have greater control on how well your investment is paying off than you would if you were to invest in stock in a company run by somebody else.

❖ *Long-term investment*: Many people like the idea of an investment that can fund their retirement. Rental housing is one sector that rarely decreases in price, making it a good option for long-term investments. Real estate will typically increase in value as time goes on, compared to a savings account that will lose value as inflation rises.

❖ *Positive cash flow*: Many real estate investments potentially offer positive monthly cash flow after your mortgage and other related expenses are paid. This cash flow will most likely increase over time as your mortgage financing decreases incrementally and rental rates increase. This will create a growing source of secure retirement income for you.

Final Thoughts

Dear Nazeefah and Nabeel,

Go forth and invest in real estate. In the future, land will become the most valuable commodity. It will become more valuable than gold, minerals, or water. Real estate is one of the safest possible investments, as long as you adopt a "buy and hold" strategy and your property generates a positive "cash flow." Own real estate. You will not be disappointed in the long term.

Love,

Dad

35

COMMON MONEY BLUNDERS YOU CAN AVOID

Don't think money does everything, or you are going to
end up doing everything for money.

— VOLTAIRE

Confession #31

As a young adult, I was not able to escape money blunders. There are too many to mention here, but the one that stands out is my "youthful arrogance" leading me to spend money like there was no tomorrow. I failed to plan for a rainy day and thought that the little money I had made me invincible. I failed to respect the number-one rule of money: "Don't spend more than you earn."

There is no substitute for experience. Successful individuals understand that they can benefit from other people's experience where their own is lacking. Even though parents and elders may seem out of touch with the modern world, they have had life experiences that no amount of education can match. While financial advisors may not have personal experience with many of the situations they advise on, they have instead gained knowledge and understanding through study, application, and mentoring on financial topics.

Thinking that you must make all your own mistakes is a form of pride that will hinder your financial goals and risk your future. Don't be stubborn! It is better to explore sound money concepts and determine whether or not they apply to your particular situation. Remember to be open-minded, and to seek answers through mentors, elders, study, blogs, publications, news, and, of course, your parents. In doing so, you will adopt strategies, personal guidelines, and solid information that will keep you on track and help you to avoid financial disasters.

Here are some tips to help you to avoid money blunders.

Don't spend more than you earn.

The math is simple—if you spend more than you earn, you will end up in debt. Refusing to spend more than you earn should be a rule that you commit to as early in life as possible.

Define your financial goals.

Don't wander around in the dark like a lost zombie! One trait successful people have in common is decisiveness. They know what they want, and they go for it. This is not to be confused with rash, impulsive decisions, of course. Defining your main financial goals and writing out the steps you will take to reach them is a way to avoid money blunders and set yourself up for success.

Don't acquire bad debt.

Be very selective about the type of debt you incur. Acquiring bad debt is a common money misstep that can change your financial standing significantly, haunting you for years to come.

Keep your credit card balance low and paid in full monthly.

Mismanaging credit cards may be the most common money blunder of all. Credit card debt can quickly become unmanageable, drastically impacting your finances. Limit your credit cards to no more than two, and pay your entire balance off each month if possible. Use the cards sparingly. Do not depend on them for monthly expenses.

Choose adequate and updated insurance coverage.

It may seem like you can't afford insurance coverage, but in most cases, you can't afford NOT to have insurance coverage! Do your due diligence when searching for health, auto, homeowner's, and renter's insurance. Evaluate your coverage every six months to make sure you are still getting the coverage that best suits your needs. Also, check for any new discounts for which you may be eligible. Auto insurance companies sometimes give rate reductions for policyholders who have no accidents within a certain period of time and for those who have multiple insurance policies with them. You may also get rate reductions at certain milestones, such as when you turn twenty-one or twenty-five. Health insurance companies sometimes offer rewards for those who adopt healthy lifestyles, like nonsmokers.

Sometimes, insurance companies and large corporations collaborate to provide special insurance discounts to employees. If you work for a large corporation and have health insurance through your employer, you may also be eligible for discounts on your homeowner's, renter's, and auto insurance, all through the same company.

Stay organized and pay bills on time.

Your creditors do not differentiate between you paying a bill late because you forgot the due date and paying it late because you did not have enough money to pay it on time. It's important to write your bills' due dates on a calendar or to set up phone reminders so that you pay every bill on time, every month. This includes bills for your utilities, credit cards, rent or mortgage, car payments, insurance payments, and any other expenses you have. Even a few late payments can affect your credit record, and you may incur fees on some late payments, even when they are only one day late.

Besides writing them on the calendar, it can be useful to coordinate due dates with your paycheck dates. If you get paid on the first and twentieth of each month, write down all of the bills you will pay on the first and all that you will pay on the twentieth. You may even find it useful and time-saving to write the checks for the whole month and keep them in an envelope until the correct date to send them.

All creditors now accept online payments. If you are forgetful (like this dad!), or have a difficult time staying organized enough to pay bills on time, setting up automatic bill pay with your bank may save you the trouble of paying them manually every month. However, you must still make sure that you have the funds in your account on the right dates to cover the auto payments. Otherwise, if your bank sends out automatic payments each month when your account lacks the necessary funds, it will charge you a hefty overdraft charge. This is another area where staying organized can save you money: in this case, by helping you to prevent unnecessary fees.

Don't cash out your retirement.

If you have contributed to a retirement fund at your job and you leave the company, you have two options. One option is to roll over the funds into another retirement account, and the other is to take the money out of the account. In most cases, it is best to roll over the money and continue to build your retirement fund. Unless you need it for something specific, you will probably never miss the money, and when it is time for you to retire you'll know you made the right decision.

Develop thrifty habits.

You may have heard stories about people who picked up pennies off sidewalks, eventually amassing thousands of dollars. These stories remind us that even a few saved pennies a day can add up over time. If you save five dollars every workday by packing a bag lunch from leftovers at home instead of eating lunch out, you could put an extra $100 per month into your savings account. Doesn't seem like much? Think again! In ten years, you will have saved $12,000 from practicing just one thrifty habit.

Lock in a low-interest mortgage.

If you choose a mortgage with a set rate lock in a low-interest mortgage, you can save thousands of dollars over the lifetime of the loan. First-time homebuyers sometimes make the mistake of thinking that an interest rate that is only a few percentage points higher does not make much difference, but it is actually quite significant! Shop wisely for a low-interest mortgage and make sure you can meet all of the qualifications.

Understand your student loans.

As you prepare for college, you may have only one thing in mind—getting the right education to enter a lucrative career. There is nothing wrong with having focused career goals unless it blinds you from the reality of student loans. Many students take out student loans without realizing what their monthly payments will be when it is time to pay back the loan. Monthly payments can be a shocker when it is time to pay back the loan with interest. Make sure you know what you are committing to before you sign on the dotted line!

Be realistic about expenses.

You have crunched the numbers. You know that if you live frugally for the next five years, you will be able to afford the $350 monthly payments for the car you want. You have written down the details for car payment and insurance for your parents, but you have glossed over some important expenses of owning and operating a car—fuel, maintenance, and repairs. Depending on how much you drive the new car, fuel bills can easily hit a few hundred dollars per month. Even if you have a good warranty and avoid repair bills for the first few years, you must still maintain your car. This means regularly scheduled oil changes, new tires, and so forth. It is unrealistic to think you do not need to factor fuel and maintenance into your monthly expenses.

The car is just one example of not fully counting every real expense in your budget. Don't fudge on adding in the little things such as a daily coffee latte break that add up to $120 per month.

Keep an emergency fund.

You cannot possibly predict when you will need money that is not in your regular budget to cover an emergency. Even if it means having to cut back in another area, feed your emergency fund every month. If possible, keep no less than three to six months of living expenses in your emergency fund. Don't forget to increase the size of your emergency fund if your monthly expenses increase.

Keep a cushion in your checking account.

Take care not to spend everything in your checking account from one paycheck to the next. Instead, leave a cushion to cover incidental expenses, ensuring you won't end up with overdraft fees if you accidentally overspend by a few dollars.

Carefully consider making personal loans and cosigning loans.

If you decide to give a friend a personal loan or cosign a loan for him or her, make sure you consider how it can affect your own finances if the loan is not paid back. Even the most reliable individuals can experience unexpected changes in their finances that prevent them from paying back a loan on time. Unfortunately, if this happens to your friend, you'll nonetheless be responsible for the loan because you gave your word (signature) that you would pay if the friend could not. Can you afford the monthly payments? If a friend does not pay back a personal loan, will it cause you to miss paying a bill on time? Most financial experts agree that it is never wise to loan money to a friend unless you can afford to lose the money — and possibly the friend.

Final Thoughts

Dear Nazeefah and Nabeel,
*   I have encouraged you to think for yourself and to be creative. However, when it comes to money, you should be prepared to learn from those who have life experiences and have been successful at managing their money and formed good habits around money.*
I'm always here for advice.
Dad

36

KEEP TABS ON YOUR FINANCIAL HEALTH

Knowing yourself is the beginning of all wisdom.

— ARISTOTLE

Confession #32

Youthful complacency and a lack of discipline impacted my ability to monitor my financial health. Tracking my finances was boring when I was young, because I was too busy spending money I did not have. I neglected to see the importance of monitoring my spending, managing my debt, and keeping track of the performance of my investments.

Performing the follow procedures regularly will allow you to keep finances in check.

Keep yourself aware of the state of your finances since you are the one in charge.

Even if you are fortunate enough to have a professional to help with your financial records and accounting, you still need to know what assets you have and where they go.

Keep good records—an absolute must when tracking your money.

Create a system for keeping receipts and records, reviewing your bills every month, and tracking spending so you can know that you're sticking to your budget.

Check your credit report at least once a year.

It is common for a person to find several mistakes added to his or her credit report each year. Sometimes, the mistakes can be costly! Your credit report needs to be accurate. Otherwise, it is not useful. If you find mistakes on your credit report, contact the credit bureau that issued the report. The Bureau will require proof of identity and proof that the disputed item on the report does not pertain to you. You may have to make several phone calls and write letters to clear the matter, but eventually you will get to the bottom of the mistake and the issue will be corrected – saving you money in the process.

Review your bank account records every month.

Spotting unusual activity as quickly as possible is critical when it comes to detecting fraudulent practices, such as identity theft and unauthorized charges. Reviewing your bank records is a simple exercise you can easily do via your smart phone.

Review your spending habits every month and make immediate adjustments as needed.

When something is awry in your finances, do not procrastinate. Be proactive! Unhealthy financial situations do not heal without your help.

Be honest with yourself about what you see.

Have the courage to change, adjust, expand, let go of unnecessary expenses, or do whatever you need to do to stay financially healthy.

Final Thoughts

Dear Nazeefah and Nabeel,

Life keeps us all busy, yet we must take the time to attend to the necessities. Monitoring your financial health is essential to peace of mind and personal growth, so just do it! Get into this habit while you are young, and it will serve you well for the rest of your life.
Always looking out for you,
Dad

37

HOW TO EASILY SAVE $1,378 EACH YEAR

Save money and money will save you.

— JAMAICAN PROVERB

Confession #33

Saving money comes easily to some people; they shop within their budget, pay their bills on time, and make sure that a portion of their paycheck always goes straight into their savings account. One of our best family moments consists of sitting around the table and guessing how much money is in each of the kids' piggy banks before breaking them open. That's when they see the fruits of their sacrifices and experience the pleasure of enjoying the money that they had forgotten about. When they were young, both of my children were great "savers." But this changed once they became older, at which point they began spending all the money they had! The thought of saving a small percentage of their allowance never crossed their mind. I am now happy that both of them have developed the habit of saving.

I came across this ingenious and simple savings plan on Facebook and it hit a nerve with me because of its sheer simplicity and ease. Here is a fun way to save $1,378 per year with very little discipline. It will allow you to change your relationship with money with very little effort.

The idea is simple. During the first week of the year, you save $1. Pretty easy! During the second week, you save $2: definitely manageable! Keep adding a dollar each week, and by the last week of the year you still only need to save $52. This adds up to $1,378 over the course of a year.

So, what's the catch?

Well, the catch is that it is easy to save for the first few weeks or months, but it becomes far more challenging to save in the later weeks. If you start in January and save $1, $2, $3, $4, and so on, your first month's savings will only be $10. However, December will require you to save over $200 in increments of $49, $50, $51, and $52.

This savings plan requires discipline and may not be sustainable because our lives are not predictable.

But wait! There is a solution if you are serious about saving money. Each month, save as much as you can, maybe $20 or $40. This will require some sacrifices, but is nonetheless doable.

Print a copy of the savings table from the website – www.confessionsofadad.ca - and place it beside your bed. Each week, save as much as you can and cross off the line that matches how much you were able to save. If one week is a little worse than the one before it, no big deal; you can rebound the next week.

Remember, the goal is to build savings in a realistic way, through the ups and downs of your life. Every week should involve some forward progress, but some weeks will be better than others. Even if you don't find the "fifty-two-week money challenge" to be particularly useful, there's still a great deal of value in keeping the principle of realistic savings in mind.

You don't have to set a new savings record every week. You just need to move forward at least a little bit all the time.

Final Thoughts

Dear Nazeefah and Nabeel,

It is important for you to develop discipline in your ability to save money. The best way to gain that discipline is to start by putting away a small amount each week, incrementally working up to saving more. Even by saving small amounts, you are creating a disciplined savings mindset. The amount is less important than the habit. As time progresses, the act of saving will become effortless, and you will look forward to financial achievement. The savings challenge is a good starting point to put away as much as you can and soon you will see your savings grow.

Through small steps, I am committed to helping you build the financial discipline that will determine the course of your future.

Best of luck,

Dad

52 Week Savings Challenge

WEEK	DEPOSIT AMOUNT	ACCOUNT BALANCE	WEEK	DEPOSIT AMOUNT	ACCOUNT BALANCE
1	$ 1.00	$ 1.00	27	$ 27.00	$ 378.00
2	$ 2.00	$ 3.00	28	$ 28.00	$ 406.00
3	$ 3.00	$ 6.00	29	$ 29.00	$ 435.00
4	$ 4.00	$ 10.00	30	$ 30.00	$ 465.00
5	$ 5.00	$ 15.00	31	$ 31.00	$ 496.00
6	$ 6.00	$ 21.00	32	$ 32.00	$ 528.00
7	$ 7.00	$ 28.00	33	$ 33.00	$ 561.00
8	$ 8.00	$ 36.00	34	$ 34.00	$ 595.00
9	$ 9.00	$ 45.00	35	$ 35.00	$ 630.00
10	$ 10.00	$ 55.00	36	$ 36.00	$ 666.00
11	$ 11.00	$ 66.00	37	$ 37.00	$ 703.00
12	$ 12.00	$ 78.00	38	$ 38.00	$ 741.00
13	$ 13.00	$ 91.00	39	$ 39.00	$ 780.00
14	$ 14.00	$ 105.00	40	$ 40.00	$ 820.00
15	$ 15.00	$ 120.00	41	$ 41.00	$ 861.00
16	$ 16.00	$ 136.00	42	$ 42.00	$ 903.00
17	$ 17.00	$ 153.00	43	$ 43.00	$ 946.00
18	$ 18.00	$ 171.00	44	$ 44.00	$ 990.00
19	$ 19.00	$ 190.00	45	$ 45.00	$ 1,035.00
20	$ 20.00	$ 210.00	46	$ 46.00	$ 1,081.00
21	$ 21.00	$ 231.00	47	$ 47.00	$ 1,128.00
22	$ 22.00	$ 253.00	48	$ 48.00	$ 1,176.00
23	$ 23.00	$ 276.00	49	$ 49.00	$ 1,225.00
24	$ 24.00	$ 300.00	50	$ 50.00	$ 1,275.00
25	$ 25.00	$ 325.00	51	$ 51.00	$ 1,326.00
26	$ 26.00	$ 351.00	52	$ 52.00	$ 1,378.00

PART FOUR: SAGE ADVICE

"Life is like a sandwich!

Birth as one slice, and death as the other.
What you put in-between the slices is up to you.

— ALLAN RUFUS

38

WEALTH LESSONS FROM VINCENT VAN GOGH

Too many people spend money they haven't earned, to buy things they don't want, to impress people they don't like.

— WILL SMITH

Vincent van Gogh was one of the greatest painters of all time. He also spent most of his life destitute. The one woman he loved rejected him. Almost everyone who saw his paintings found very little value in them, and he was never seen as a talented painter.

Historians have characterized Van Gogh as somebody struggling with self-doubt and physical and mental challenges. They also depict him as a person with passion and drive and a sense that he was doing the right thing even when the people around him didn't believe in him.

Why am I telling you about somebody who died in the nineteenth century? I always try to learn from successful people (whether or not their success brought wealth), applying their lessons to my own life. Van Gogh was not financially free, nor was he a real estate investor. In fact, he had no money and was dependent on his brother. However, I have gleaned many lessons from his life that I continue to apply today.

Don't make choices to please other people.

Don't buy stuff because other people want you to buy stuff. Don't spend money because other people want you to spend money.

Make your own financial decisions and don't feel bad about making different choices.

If you find that your values are deviating from the crowd, don't be afraid to start seeking out new people to spend your time with.

Life is a marathon, not a sprint.

The people that succeed are the people who keep moving toward their goals. If you want to find financial success, you must accept that it won't happen tomorrow or the day after that. For most people, real financial success will take years to find. The same is true for career success, entrepreneurial success, and even relationship success. A quick-fix solution will rarely build long-term value or financial freedom.

Doubting yourself is normal.

Everyone feels doubt. Even people who seem extremely confident or portray great financial success through their possessions are often just wearing a public face. There will be times where you feel as though you're not doing the right thing. Financial freedom means different things to different people. You have to define what it means to you.

You don't need material stuff to have a successful life.

Van Gogh's example is an extreme one, but there's still something to be learned there. He didn't live a life filled with possessions, yet his life changed the world.

Final Thoughts

Make it your goal in life to learn lessons from people from all walks of life. Learn lessons from everybody, and from every situation. Learn from history and from successful people. Use the good advice you receive, and discard what does not appeal to you.

39

TO LOAN OR NOT TO LOAN

Before borrowing money from a friend, decide which you
need most.

— PROVERB

Confession #34

*I have no problem helping people when they are in difficulty. There is no better feeling
than to lend friends and family money when they need help. However, I got "burned"
and lost a friendship when a good friend delayed paying me back a loan on grounds that
he could not afford to do so. In the process, I learned a very hard lesson and decided to
follow the following guidelines before giving anybody a loan.*

Some people have a strict policy about never loaning money to friends
or family members, and they stick to that policy no matter the circumstances. These people may have learned the hard way that loans to friends
or family members can create sticky situations. Even worse, many family
feuds have started and friends have been lost over loans.

Rarely are things so cut and dry that one can adopt a strict policy to
adhere to without fail. There are usually exceptions. Sometimes policies
are broken simply because one knows the policy goes against what is the

right thing for that moment, case, or person. This is often the case in these matters.

The first thing you should determine in deciding whether to loan to family members or friends is whether you actually have the money to loan them without jeopardizing your own finances, plans, or responsibilities. In other words, if the loan is not paid back on time, would it affect your ability to pay your bills or take care of responsibilities? Will it affect others if the loan is not paid back on time? For instance, suppose you have saved money to go on a trip with a friend and planned to share travel and lodging costs together. Now – what if you've already loaned your travel money to another friend who doesn't give it back on time: is your vacation partner going to be left holding the bag – literally – if you can't go?

No matter how well you know a friend, and no matter how firmly you believe you can count on him or her to pay the money back, bad things happen to good people. For one reason or another, it's possible your friend may not be able to pay the loan back. If this happens, what will your attitude be? Will you become angry and resentful? Will it ruin your friendship? Will you hang it over your friend's head for the rest of your days? Or are you the kind of person who can forgive, forget, and move on?

Some say you should not loan money to anyone unless you can afford to give away the money. When you take this approach, if the money is not paid back, you will not be upset because you are considering the loan a gift. If the person does insist on paying it back, you will have bonus money that you can invest or pay forward. It's a win-win situation.

If you have the means to help a friend or family member who needs a loan but cannot obtain the loan through traditional sources, you can treat the loan as a business deal. Write a contract that specifies both the loan amount, as well as when and how the loan will be paid back. Explain that you have the expectation that the loan will be paid back per the written agreement. Make sure the person understands the terms of the loan. I prefer not to charge any interest on the loan because it is not correct to take advantage of anybody in a desperate situation.

Final Thoughts

Dear Nazeefah and Nabeel,

As you get older, there will come a time when a friend or a loved one is in a difficult situation and will come to you for help. Deciding whether or not to loan money to your loved ones can be a difficult choice to make. In the end, however, it comes down to who you are and whether or not you can afford to do it. Keep in mind that when you loan money, you are taking a risk. Ask yourself if you're willing to risk the money and the friend. Don't be greedy or selfish with what you have. But at the same time, don't be a fool and let people take advantage of you, either.

Use your heart when you are lending out money — but don't forget to use your mind, too.

Dad

40

YES...MAYBE...NO...JUST MAKE THE DECISION

> Whenever you see a successful business, someone once
> made a courageous decision.
>
> — PETER F. DRUCKER

Confession #35

*I used to suffer from analysis paralysis. I remember how I second-guessed myself before
purchasing a computer — I could not decide between a PC or a Mac. I overanalyzed and
agonized over the decision until I was paralyzed and could not make a decision at all.
And this was only over a computer. In the end, I didn't decide for six months.*

In our lives, there are many financial decisions to be made. Sometimes
it is clear that one decision is wrong and one is right based on our moral
beliefs and values. Sometimes we don't struggle with making a decision
at all. Whether it comes from the teaching we received as children, from
something we heard someone say, or is simply a result of thinking intently
about it, we just automatically know the right thing to do.

Other decisions are not so easy to make. Often, there doesn't seem to
be a clear-cut answer. One way seems as right or wrong as the other.

Uncertainty can torment us, taunting us to go one way in one moment and the other the next. Author Lisa Wingate says in her book *A Month of Summer*, "The hardest thing about the road not taken is that you never know where it might have led." We sometimes become afraid that whichever road we choose, we will miss something on the road we don't take. Yet we have to muster the courage to choose one of the roads: we can't travel them both at the same time! So how do we make a quality decision?

Let's assume you are thinking of purchasing your first car, a very big decision if you are in your twenties. Here are some steps that will help you through the financial decision-making process.

Clearly define the decision.

What exactly do you need to decide? What do you need the car for? How much can you spend? Do you need to make a decision right away or do you have some time?

Gather as much information as you can

How much will it cost me for gas? What about maintenance? Can I afford insurance coverage?

Throw out any unrealistic or unusable solutions.

Discard anything that is not in tune with your values or lifestyle. A fancy sports car would be nice to have, but is clearly unrealistic at this time. This will help clear your mind for possibilities.

Weigh the pros and cons.

On a sheet of paper make two columns and list the pros and cons of each possible solution. Is a used car a more affordable option, or is public transport the more viable choice?

If appropriate, seek advice from professionals or trusted friends.

Sometimes you may be too close to the situation to see the answer objectively. Speak to car owners, mechanics, and insurance companies. Having an outside perspective can help you see things that you could not see before.

Once you make a choice, stick with it unless you have a compelling reason to abandon it and make a different choice.

Final Thoughts

Dear Nazeefah and Nabeel,

You will have to make many difficult decisions over the course of your life. Collect information, and bite the bullet. Financial decisions can be scary, but you will learn to trust yourself to make quality decisions that are not based on fear.

As Canadian hockey legend, Wayne Gretzky, said, "You will miss 100 percent of the shots you don't take."

Once you get started making decisions, it gets easier and easier as you gradually learn what it is you are looking for.

Yours,

Dad

41

FINANCIAL LESSONS I LEARNED FROM MY KIDS

While we try to teach our children all about life, our children teach us what life is all about.

— Angela Schwind

Throughout the book I have tried to impart lessons to my kids about the value of money based on some of the things they have taught me. I would be amiss if I did not speak about the financial lessons that they in turn have taught me.

Those who know Nabeel are aware that he loves technology, especially Apple products. A year before the iPad was launched, he planned to save for the "coolest, best and greatest Apple gadget ever." He really wanted this gadget!

Instead of insisting that we purchase it for him, Nabeel did some research. He determined how much it would cost and then calculated how many allowances, birthday gifts, and other gifts he'd have to save in order to afford it.

He patiently saved his allowance for a year, sacrificed his birthday party and birthday gifts, collected spare change stuck in the sofa, and somehow managed to convince his sister to part with her spare change for this "worthy cause." When the iPad was launched, he happily went to the store and bought himself one. I couldn't have been prouder.

No, I'm not proud because he got an iPad. I'm proud for other reasons.

❖ I'm proud that he didn't simply ask for or expect his parents to buy the iPad for him.
❖ I'm proud that he knew to save diligently for it and not to spend money along the way.
❖ I'm proud that even though he was saving for the iPad, he set a goal for himself and sacrificed to achieve his goal.

When Nazeefah received her first credit card at age seventeen, I sat down with her and explained the ins and outs together with the responsibilities of owning a credit card. You shouldn't have a balance owed at the end of the month, I explained, and you shouldn't withdraw cash from your credit line, but you *should* use it as a tool of convenience when you purchase on-line items. Even though I preached the proper use of credit cards, I knew deep down that I would have to "bail her out" because she would overextend herself—it was just a matter of time.

I am proud to say that over the past four years, I have not bailed her out of her credit card payments once. Shocker for me! I was even more impressed at how she diligently paid the bills on her card, in full, every month. This meant that she incurred zero, nada, zilch interest payments since she started using the card. Wow! I cannot even claim to have done that with *my* credit card.

So, what financial lessons did I learn?

❖ First, I learned that our kids had listened (to my surprise, shock, and horror!) when we gave them advice. They followed our example without understanding why. They trusted us and innocently assumed that it was the right thing to do.

❖ Second, I found out that they understood that everything costs money that Mom and Dad have to work to earn. They also tuned into the fact that the more money they spend, the harder Mom and Dad have to work.

❖ Third, I saw that I had underestimated the value of leading by example. Kids observe the people around them with enthusiastic intensity. They typically mimic the actions that work and ignore the ones that don't.

Final Thoughts

If you want your kids to learn how to save, lead by example. Get them started young, and demonstrate discipline and diligence.

42

MUST-READ PERSONAL FINANCE BOOKS

> When I get a little money, I buy books. If any is left, I buy
> food and clothes.
>
> — ERASMUS

Knowledge is indeed power! I have taken my inspiration from authors I admire and books that hold messages that will live forever. Over the course of your life, read or listen to the following books. They changed my life and they will change yours, too.

The Wealthy Barber

One of the first personal finance books I read was *The Wealthy Barber* by Canadian author, Dragon's Den investor, and someone I personally admire, David Chilton. In his book, Chilton tells the story of how he and his siblings learned about financial management from Roy, a local barber who achieved financial success through following simple planning concepts. Chilton provides his readers with straightforward, realistic financial guidelines and strategies for planning real-life examples. The book is filled with sensible money management advice and is a very funny read.

Best quote: "You hate to begin with a harsh dose of reality, but here it goes: Unless you marry into wealth or come from a well-to-do family (both highly advisable strategies, by the way), you'll have to learn to spend less than you make."

The Richest Man in Babylon

George S. Clason's parables about acquiring wealth have inspired investors since the 1920s. Like most of the personal finance books that have followed, *The Richest Man in Babylon* emphasizes saving over spending. However, the book also insists that charitable giving is equally as important, provided you don't allow those to whom you give to become dependent upon your gifts.

Best quote: "Budget thy expenses that thou mayest have coins to pay for thy necessities, to pay for thy enjoyments and to gratify thy worthwhile desires without spending more than nine-tenths of thy earnings."

Rich Dad, Poor Dad

This is the story of author Robert Kiyosaki's upbringing in Hawaii and of his two fathers—one rich (not biological) and one poor (biological). Kiyosaki was forced to choose between following in the footsteps of his poor father—a highly educated government worker—or his rich father—an entrepreneur who never graduated from high school.

Ultimately, Kiyosaki decides to learn from his rich dad. The book focuses mostly on the education and financial advice Kiyosaki learned from this dad. His rich father was able to create a multimillion-dollar empire from virtually nothing, using only his financial acumen and the power of his imagination.

Best quote: "The key to financial freedom and great wealth is a person's ability or skill to convert earned income into passive income."

The Millionaire Next Door

The general premise of *The Millionaire Next Door* is that the pop culture concept of a millionaire is quite false, and that most actual millionaires live a very simple lifestyle. The authors, Thomas Stanley and William Danko, did extensive profiling of individuals whose net worth defined them as millionaires, along with those whose salaries and age defined them as people who would likely become millionaires. Using this data, they created a detailed profile of who exactly a typical millionaire is. From there, they conducted extensive interviews with these "typical" millionaires to create a much more detailed picture of what it actually means to be a millionaire in today's society.

Best quote: "Those whom we define as being wealthy get much more pleasure from owning substantial amounts of appreciable assets than from displaying a high-consumption lifestyle"

Think and Grow Rich

Think and Grow Rich is a blueprint for achieving wealth and personal success. Instead of discussing how to start a business or invest money, the book focuses on the psychological, emotional, and spiritual growth required for financial achievement.

The book uses the material Hill collected over many years of interviewing successful people, synthesizing it into a philosophy of success. It contains the personal stories and anecdotes of early-twentieth-century millionaires, including Woodrow Wilson, Thomas Edison, John D. Rockefeller, Henry Ford, and Alexander Graham Bell.

Along with the personal stories of successful businessmen, the book provides steps to developing each of the attributes necessary for success.

Best quote: "If you truly desire money so keenly that your desire is an obsession, you will have no difficulty in convincing yourself that you will acquire it. The object is to want money, and to be so determined to have it that you convince yourself that you will have it."

The Automatic Millionaire

The Automatic Millionaire is based on sound financial concepts. The author encourages readers to eliminate debt, live frugally, and pay themselves first. But the message of his book is unique: Rather than develop willpower and self-discipline, David Bach says, why not bypass the human element altogether? Why not make your path to wealth automatic?

Bach delivers a practical, straightforward guide to financial security that starts and ends with the maxim "Pay yourself first." Before worrying about taxes or investing or budgeting, focus on paying yourself for the work you do every day by putting it aside to be accessed later. He emphasizes the importance of using automated payroll deductions to avoid the temptation of using savings to pay today's bills.

Best quote: "Most people believe that the secret to getting rich is all about finding ways of increasing their income as quickly as possible. 'If only I could make more money,' they declare, 'I'd be rich.' How many times have you heard somebody say that? How many times have you said it yourself? Well, it simply isn't true. Ask anyone who got a raise last year if their savings increased. In almost every case, the answer will be no. Why? Because more often than not, the more we make, the more we spend."

The Behavior Gap: Simple Ways to Stop Doing Dumb Things with Money

As a financial planner, Carl Richards grew frustrated watching people he cared about make the same mistakes over and over with their money. They were letting emotion get in the way of making smart financial decisions. He called this phenomenon—involving a distance between what we should do and what we actually do—"the behavior gap." Using simple drawings to explain the gap, he found that once people understood it, they started doing much better.

Best quote: "We've all made mistakes, but now it's time to give yourself permission to review those mistakes, identify your personal behavior gaps, and make a plan to avoid them in the future. The goal isn't to make the 'perfect' decision about money every time, but to do the best we can and move forward. Most of the time that's enough..."

I Will Teach You to Be Rich

This book is aimed at twenty- to thirty-five-year-olds, and it's essentially a guide to getting your finances on track. Author Ramit Sethi's six-week personal finance program teaches you how to automate savings and jumpstart investing, and includes more than a little information on banking, budgeting, and entrepreneurship along the way. Sethi's completely practical approach is delivered with a nonjudgmental style that makes readers want to do what he says. It is based around the four pillars of personal finance—banking, saving, budgeting, and investing—and the wealth-building ideas of personal entrepreneurship.

Best quote: "Our education system doesn't teach this,' people whine. It's easy for people in their twenties to wish that their colleges had offered some personal-finance training. Guess what? Most colleges do offer those classes. You just didn't attend!"

Debt Is Slavery

Author Michael Mihalik's short book is packed with sensible advice about money, offering preventative tips for students and young adults plus a concise treatment for anyone struggling with debt. He created a short read that gets right to the point. He offers practical advice and illustrates financial concepts with relevant examples.

Best quote: "Do you ever wake up in the morning and groan, 'I don't want to go to work today?' As you lie in bed toying with the idea of staying home, your thoughts turn to all the bills you have to pay. So you drag your tired self out of your warm bed, drink a pot of coffee, and drive to work (in your cool car—only 43 more payments and that baby is all yours!). You drag yourself out of bed and go to work, because you have to. Isn't that a form of slavery?"

Final Thoughts

Seek (financial) knowledge. Seek it often, and apply what you have learned.

43

FINAL THOUGHTS ON MONEY

It's just money.

The worst thing to teach your kids about money is that it's only green paper. Money is required for existence in society. However, it cannot buy love, friends, or happiness. Nor will they take it with them after their life is over.

Take responsibility for educating your kids about finance.

In a poll of parents by the website iVillage.com, 65 percent state that their own parents had taught them nothing about money. This would explain a portion of the current debt crisis. It is parent's responsibility to mentor their children in the important facts of life. Money stands tall on that list.

Start teaching kids about money at a young age.

Kindergarten-age children are fascinated with money. Isn't it refreshing to see a person get truly excited over a nickel? Teaching children this age about money also comes with the extra benefit of teaching them math skills. Introduce them to all of the different-valued coins. Have them count and divide them. They will never tire of this game!

Teach your children financial common sense.

Scott Reeves of *Forbes* magazine writes, "If you can teach your child the difference between needs and wants, how to budget and how to save, your child will know more than many adults." Proper money management is basically just about having common sense and keeping our greed in check.

Exert counterinfluence on social messages.

We live in a consumer-based economy. Our current system only works when people spend great deals of money. We also have to contend with daily bombardment from advertising. Children are encouraged to want and to spend from an early age. You can counteract this influence by teaching them the skills for a properly-balanced life, and that starts with you demonstrating contentment.

Final Thoughts

When it comes to money, you can't win. If you focus on making it, you're materialistic. If you try to but don't make any, you're a loser. If you make a lot and keep it, you're a miser. If you make it and spend it, you're a spendthrift. If you don't care about making it, you're unambitious. If you make a lot and still have it when you die, you're a fool—for trying to take it with you. The only way to really win with money is to hold it loosely—and be generous with it to accomplish things of value.

—John C. Maxwell

Give.

Routine, structure, and consistency.

Always spend less than you earn.

Think before you spend.

Eliminate debt.

Freedom is your goal.

Understand where your money goes.

Live with integrity, and value your character.

Remembering a simple acronym can sum up the advice in this book: GRATEFUL, referring to the following ideas.

Give generously.

Give with no strings attached, and expect nothing in return.

Routines are the key.

In your daily routine, you should minimize the amount of money you spend. Every time you can find a way to reduce spending as part of your normal routine, you should take advantage of it. Shaving off just a few cents a day from your routine adds up greatly over time. That extra dollar you spend every day adds up to $365 by the end of the year. Experiment with little changes that you can make to your day. Cut your spending until you can reach a way to maintain the life you want to lead while minimizing daily expenses. You'll never regret it.

Always spend less than you earn.

No matter what you earn, you need to strive to spend less than that amount. You should never spend more than your pay check, because, if you do, you're either depleting your savings or relying on credit, both of which are financially disastrous over the long run. If you know big expenses are coming up, put aside some cash right now to help deal with them later.

Think before you spend.

Take a moment to evaluate your purchases before you make them. Thirty seconds of intelligent thought could prevent a world of dumb mistakes.

Eliminate debt.

Enough said.

Freedom is your goal.

Decide what financial freedom means to you. Do everything you can to not lose that freedom.

Understand where your money goes.

Creating and building wealth requires an awareness of where you spend your money.

Live with integrity and value your character.

All you have is your character. It takes years to build up a reputation. But it can be tarnished in seconds.

FINAL ADVICE FROM A FATHER

I believe that what we become depends on what our fathers teach us at odd moments, when they aren't trying to teach us. We are formed by little scraps of wisdom.

— UMBERTO ECO, *FOUCAULT'S PENDULUM*

To conclude this book, the following descriptions contain simple but profound advice on matters critical for financial success. Let them be a checklist of sorts. Here's to success in all you do!

Stay away from debt.

Make an effort to not owe money to anybody. Do not pay interest on anything that you can afford to pay cash for. Make sure that 10 percent of your salary goes toward your savings account.

Pay bills first.

Do not entertain the thought of using bill money for other things. When you get paid, pay the bills. It's as simple as that.

Think about your finances every day.

Keep your drive to succeed in your mind. Putting your finances on the back burner for too long can be destructive.

Budgeting is not a bad word.

Setting boundaries for yourself is a necessary part of living a responsible life.

Invest in real estate.

Everybody needs a place to live.

Be realistic.

Numbers don't lie. Financial reports don't lie. Face the music. Don't kid yourself. Remain realistic when assessing your spending, your giving, and your income.

Spend money on experiences, not things.

Your most valuable assets are things that cannot be bought. These assets include your relationship with your significant other, children, family members, and friends. Use your money to create memories and good times. Experiences with the people you love are meaningful, fulfilling, and can last a lifetime.

Be satisfied with living a normal life.

Somewhere along the line, our society came to believe that everyone is entitled to an extraordinary life of leisure and luxury. Both those with money and those without have the expectation of easy lives, abundant material possessions, a lavish lifestyle, and instant gratification. This is an unrealistic expectation. This is not real life. It's important to be content with a normal life. You are only granted one life, so live it in the moment and live without regret. It's *your* life. It is precious and worth living.

Enter into all financial matters with your eyes open.

It's your responsibility to learn the things you need in order to manage your finances and navigate transactions. Always understand contracts before signing. Know how to read financial records. Know and understand financial terms.

Never use money to camouflage your insecurities.

Love your work. If you ever choose to take a well-paying job that you hate over a job you love that pays little, you will regret taking the job you hate. When you can, do what you love and live on a tighter budget.

Live honestly and let your lifestyle reflect a commitment to helping others.

Listen to Brian Tracey's statement "Today the greatest single source of wealth is between your ears." Think! Be smart in your finances. If you do not use intelligence in your finances, the amount of money you acquire will not matter at all.

People are the most important thing in our lives. Never lose sight of that.

Final Thoughts

Dear Nazeefah and Nabeel,

I could write many more books and never come close to sharing all the financial information with you that I would like to. To sum up, the path to success is paved with a small number of simple rules. There are no guarantees, but if you follow the rules, you are likely to achieve what you want in life.

Most people are fighting the same financial battles. We're all tempted to buy things we don't need, with money we don't have to impress people we don't like. We all struggle with spending less than we earn and creating a secure and happy life.

We all make mistakes. We all fall short of our goals. We all fall into traps and pitfalls — and sometimes those traps and pitfalls are quite deep.

Sometimes, we pick up the ball and run. Sometimes, we miss the boat.

Yes, some of us earn more than others, but so many of our choices and so many of the challenges are exactly the same.

I set out to write this book so that you could have a roadmap to follow, helping you stay on course during your life. I am grateful to be able to pass my knowledge on to you, and will continue to share tools and tips to help you along the way. I hope this book is a small start to many interesting conversations to come. There is no one with whom I would rather share my knowledge with than with the two of you.

With a deep belief in the success of your financial future.

All my love,

Dad